George Shea

Memoir Concerning the Seabury Commemoration Held at Saint Paul's Cathedral, London

Vol. 1

George Shea

Memoir Concerning the Seabury Commemoration Held at Saint Paul's Cathedral, London

Vol. 1

ISBN/EAN: 9783337428273

Printed in Europe, USA, Canada, Australia, Japan

Cover: Foto ©Lupo / pixelio.de

More available books at **www.hansebooks.com**

MEMOIR

CONCERNING

THE SEABURY COMMEMORATION

HELD AT

ST PAUL'S CATHEDRAL, LONDON

THE FOURTEENTH DAY OF NOVEMBER, A. D. 1884

PRINTED CHIEFLY FROM A MANUSCRIPT MONOGRAPH INTRO-
DUCTORY TO A UNIQUE VOLUME IN THE POSSESSION

OF

GEORGE SHEA

THE PAGES OF WHICH ARE INSET WITH ALL THE ORIGINAL
CORRESPONDENCE AND OTHER PROOF OF
THAT HISTORICAL EVENT

BOSTON AND NEW YORK
HOUGHTON, MIFFLIN AND COMPANY
The Riverside Press, Cambridge
1893

Contents

	PAGE
LIKENESS of Bishop Seabury: facsimile of Sharp's engraving from the painting by Duché. The original portrait is at Trinity College, Hartford, Connecticut . . . . . . *Frontispiece*	
Memoir of the subject of this book	7–33
Letter from Charles Wordsworth, Bishop of St. Andrews, to George Shea	39
Letter to Dean Church, and the advisory monograph, enclosed therein, prepared at suggestion of Canon Liddon, and sent in triplicate to the Archbishop of Canterbury, Dean Church and Canon Liddon	40–51
Letter from Dean Church to George Shea, and the note, enclosed therein, from the Archbishop .	51, 52
Letters from Assistant Bishop Henry Codman Potter to George Shea	52, 54
Letter from George Shea to Bishop Horatio Potter	52–53
Letters from Canon Liddon to George Shea	54–55, 59–60
Letters from George Shea to Dean Church	40–51, 55–56
Letters from Dean Church to George Shea	51, 56, 57–58
Psalms, Lessons and Collects selected by Canon Liddon specially for the occasion	57
Letter from W. J. Seabury to George Shea .	58–59
The "interpolated" title-page to the "Form of Service"	61
Sermon by the Archbishop of Canterbury . .	63–82

Contents

Chart of Episcopal Successions from A. D. 1518 to
A. D. 1887, by Rev. W. J. Seabury, D. D. . . 84

The "Concordat" between the Scotch Bishops and
Bishop Seabury 85–89

Extract from Register at Lambeth Palace relating
to the "Scots Episcopacy as connected with the
English Episcopacy" 90

List of the Consecration and Succession of Bishops
so far as that of Seabury is concerned . . 91–97

Certificate by the "Scots Bishops" to Bishop Seabury of his consecration 98

Memoir

"MARK, NOW, HOW A PLAIN TALE SHALL PUT THEE DOWN."
Admonition to Falstaff,
Henry IV., Part I., Act II., Scene 4.

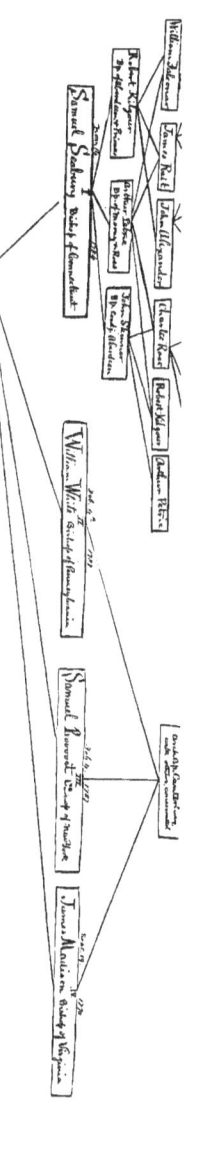

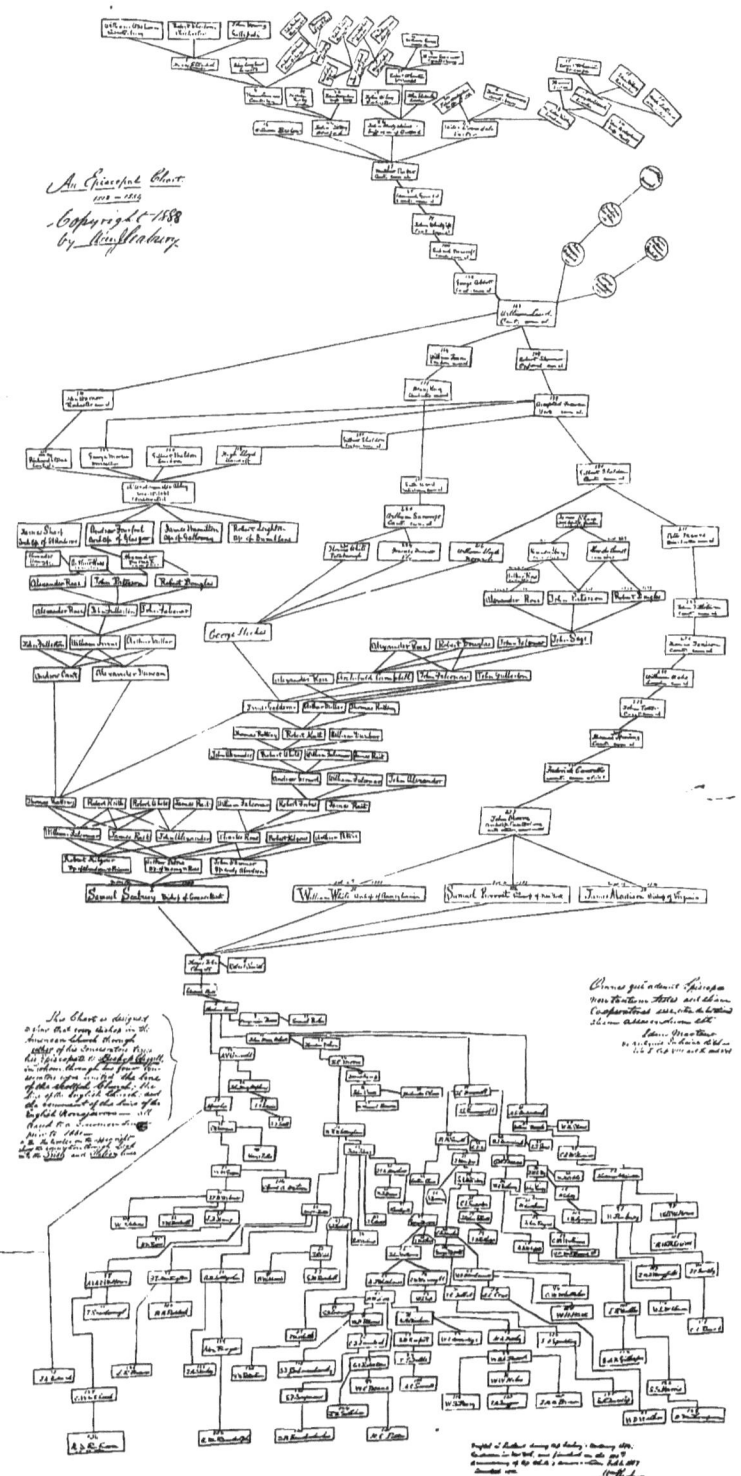

Vincit Veritas

TO record the true history and to preserve the evidences of a great event in our ecclesiastic progress I write this essay.

On Trinity Sunday, A. D. 1884, I was in Oxford, England; and, on the afternoon of that day, called upon Canon LIDDON at Christ Church. I arrived the day before at Liverpool from New York. On my way to London, I stopped at Oxford to confer with him on a subject which occupied my thought very much: in which I desired to interest him; and, through him, Canon GREGORY, his senior associate canon at St. Paul's Cathedral. I had known Dr. LIDDON since the early part of the summer of 1870, from that time had often enjoyed his hospitality, and was frequently his correspondent. On coming to Christ Church I went directly, and unannounced, to his rooms; in response to my knock it chanced that he himself, being alone, came to the outer door. Kindly recognizing me, he, in that hearty manner which he indulged towards some friends when his natural shyness had worn away, took my hand warmly in both of his, and led me into the interior room — his study. I had evidently interrupted him at work. He afterwards mentioned, in excuse for not asking me to spend the evening with him, that he had been preparing the customary discourse which he delivered each Sunday evening in term-time to a selection of students. When we were seated, I, without delay, began by telling him that my visit at this time had more purpose than only a friendly call: for I wished to consult him about a special service which I was convinced should be held, and in St. Paul's Cathedral, upon the occasion, which would occur the coming autumn, of the centennial anniversary of the consecration of SAMUEL SEABURY by the Scotch Bishops. Canon LIDDON said he was acquainted with the memorable event itself and its importance, and was conscious of the misconceived policy, influenced by political prejudices, which justified SEABURY in seeking consecration of the Scotch Church; but declared that he needed more information, and feared that others he should have to consult were no better instructed than himself. What he said was to that effect. This was not unforeseen by me: because I had often before found how little certainty of knowledge even those who were most friendly in England to The Church in America had of its history, or of our national affairs or polity. Yet Canon LIDDON had more information of those subjects than many others of our Anglican well-wishers. Nevertheless, upon this apparent invitation from him I developed my motives at full and most earnestly; first alluding to the commemorative celebration then preparing by the Scotch Church to be held at Aberdeen on October 5–8. I tried to explain that this could not meet the "opportunity" which it seemed to me the anniversary offered to The Church of England, and to her alone. I then alluded to the consecrations at Lambeth of Bishops WHITE and PROVOOST, and to the probability, if my suggestion was not acted upon, that those Anglican consecrations would be commemorated as the most important events, and become as if admittedly the primal and true initiative of the American episcopate. To allow this error to be asserted would, I suggested, be simply unhistorical, and, also, once more evince the weakness of 1784; but that a commemoration at St. Paul's, of the Aberdeen "fact," would be an acknowledgment and a sanction of the Scotch consecration, and would asseverate the independence of The Church from affairs essentially those of civil discord, and bring at once into a manifestation and declaration of unity the Churches of Scotland, England, and America. Let me be entirely candid, I said; our purpose should be to subordinate all other things attending the event to the object of bringing those churches together on November 14, under the dome of the Metropolitan Cathedral of St. Paul's, and thereby to declare their unity, and the heroic act of SEABURY and of the three Scotch Bishops. Strifes of the State need never be causes for schisms in the Church. I added, that the thought of such a celebration so far was entirely my own; and, indeed, was mainly the motive for my present visit to Europe; that it had not been suggested to me by any one; and that I meant it to be wholly individual,[1] because then the matter could be considered without embarrassment. If nothing came of my suggestion, it need not become known to others, and no cause for offence could arise. But I earnestly dwelt upon the thought that the significance of the demonstration would have a depth and certainty of purport and an influence beyond what we could now foresee or calculate; and, in conclusion, I ventured to say that the anniversary and its appropriate celebration could be fitly made "a Day of Atonement." This is the substance of my response to Canon LIDDON; and this relation contains many phrases which I uttered.

Canon LIDDON still encouraging me, I continued to develop the subject more and more and into details for the commemorative service, till the afternoon was far gone; and till it appeared to us that the project was sufficiently considered for our own preliminary uses. He promised finally, that he would call, in London, upon Canon GREGORY, as Canon GREGORY was to be during November in residence; and he repeated that they would have to depend on me for the historical particulars. From this request, repeated, I engaged to write a memoir[2] covering

---

[1] Appendix, pp. 42, 53.

[2] The memoir, written by me after my return to New York, will be seen in Appendix, pp. 41-51.

the affair, its circumstances, and some of its effects; for at that time I was hoping that he might be the preacher; afterwards I was convinced that he would have favorably entertained the proposal.

It interests me to recall — it may interest many others to learn of — incidents which occurred at this remarkable interview. The current of our after conversation carried us to reminiscences of PUSEY, KEBLE, and NEWMAN. On the mantel-piece before us in the study was a miniature bust of NEWMAN. PUSEY died since I was last at Oxford. After a while I asked Canon LIDDON how he got on with the "Life of Pusey." He replied — and it appeared to me sadly — that he had given it up; but hoped to find another hand to which it might be committed. To bring into two volumes all that should be written — which would, he said, be necessary to ensure the work being read — he had found required efforts to which his strength was not equal. The subject and its relations, he remarked, grew on him, and the need for terseness throughout the work was absolute. I felt that a great disappointment was to fall upon the religious and the literary worlds, and promptly responded: Then publish the manuscript in its present state, and let the work not be finished by any other writer. The subject of PUSEY and his times itself is interesting, but most so to a generation which is nearly passed away: the present takes little interest in it; and you yourself know and feel that the name of PUSEY is not always acceptable to a large number of our church-folk. Your own desire is that PUSEY shall become truly known and justly esteemed. Your name as the author is required to win a successful circulation, certainly in America; and there you will have a multitude of readers in and outside our own communion. I spoke to that effect, and generally those phrases were used by me. I thought I might have given offence; but, after a few moments' silence and apparently of reflection, he arose, opened one of the drawers in one of the library tables, and, taking in his hand three or four packages of manuscript, folded in oblong, told me they were chapters of the "Life of Pusey," and were as far as he had finished. It appeared to me that a great deal of work was accomplished. He then opened another drawer, and placed in my hand a package: this was of a large number of letters. They were the originals of correspondence between PUSEY and NEWMAN. He said that he was indebted to the Cardinal himself for them. Whether he told me that these letters were received through Dean CHURCH, or I supposed that they were, I am not able to recollect. I was aware — as who is not who knew either of them? — of the life-long and affectionate friendship between CHURCH and NEWMAN. I read none, indeed I opened none, of the letters. Canon LIDDON became very animated as he mentioned that they would shed "a welcome light" upon the thoughts, motives, and actions of the men of the Tractarian Movement. As he replaced the packages in the drawers he said: "Will you come with me? I hope we can get into St. Friedswide's. We have enough time before I must meet the scholars." As we passed out into the quadrangle of Christ Church the twilight was already deepening. Canon LIDDON got the key at one of the offices; we continued on our way to the entrance of the Abbey Church, where he unlocked and opened the "wicket." Our conversation ceased. I followed. We soon stood at the foot of the slab which, in the middle aisle, covers the grave of PUSEY. With closed eyes he remained a few moments in recollections or silent prayer. KEBLE, NEWMAN, PUSEY, CHURCH, LIDDON, and others of that remarkable consociation, were truly of a brotherhood of love and devotion, and more than one incident has evinced that, with them, theological adversities could not supersede the sincerities due to ancient friendship. Canon LIDDON and I went up to and I sat in the stall in the chancel where PUSEY sat during public services, and where he always used the Testament in the Greek tongue; and thence we proceeded to the pulpit from which he delivered (May, 1843) the sermon for which he was, as for heresy, suspended from preaching for two years. During this part of our visit Canon LIDDON was even more animated and very communicative. I perceived that the theme of PUSEY was losing none of its influence over his mind and heart.

We walked together toward the gateway under the great tower, and as we neared it he directed my attention to a little doorway on our left and in that corner of the quadrangle. That doorway led to the apartments which PUSEY occupied during his latter years, and there he died in an upper chamber. It was from the window of that chamber that WOLSEY watched and directed the dilapidation of the lower part of the nave of St. Friedswide's, to make larger space for the construction of what was to be known as The Cardinal's College. I had met PUSEY, in 1870, at the inauguration of Keble College; and we had afterwards written communications with each other. Canon LIDDON came with me to the street in front of the tower; again, in that familiar way of which I have spoken, he took my right hand in both of his, and said: I shall not abandon it; you have given me reasons; I shall try to finish my work. Those were his very words, I think: surely it was what he said to me. I did not speak. I could not. There and then we parted. I walked quickly to the High Street. I did not look back; I felt as if he yet stood where we had parted. I remembered long afterwards and distinctly the impression which saddened me, that we were not in this life to meet again. There was about him a lassitude and look of exhaustion which I never before noticed in him. Though we met no more, he continued to send to me by recurring opportunities kind messages and a few letters.

The next morning I proceeded by an early train up to London. On the way, further reflection determined me without delay to call upon the Very Reverend Dean CHURCH; and request him to interest the Archbishop of Canterbury. To see the Dean was, of course, in my plan from the first; but the Archbishop was a new idea, and one which might effect a change in the programme for the commemoration. I called at the Deanery, near Doctors' Commons, the following day. The Dean was on the Continent. When I returned to London, in July, he was at home. I was known to him since August, 1872. We first met at the house of a dear common friend; I had shared his hospitality; and many letters, chiefly on literary and social topics, had passed between us. I knew that I could, and I did with little preface, open the subject to him. Thoughts and sentiments habitual to him, and which were inspired by the dearest and ancient associations of his life, must, I was sure, give a welcome reception to such a proposition as that which I was to offer. I found a ready and soon an eager auditor. It was clear from his animated manner, unusual to his calm repose, that the affair had his enthusiastic sympathy. He certainly infused me with his own enthusiasm and increased mine; and I now remember, though it did not awake my full attention at the time, that we together walked the room during the greater part of our conference. As I proceeded in enforcing the opportunity for the Church of England and its duty, he several times ejaculated, *Noblesse oblige*. Dean CHURCH'S imaginative faculty was strong, fine, and delicate; he was by nature a poet; he was a clear and comprehensive thinker; and no person who learned how he stood by NEWMAN, rather in honest justice than mere friendship, in the days of tribulation at Oxford, especially in February, 1845, his proctor's year, could have doubted that he had "the courage of his convictions." Conciliatory, but uncompromising; gentle, but firm; sincerity, simplicity of feeling and of life, a sense of the awfulness of things unseen, were the characteristics of RICHARD WILLIAM CHURCH.

I told him of my visit to Canon LIDDON; and repeated to him that the thought of such a commemoration was my own, and had occurred to no one but myself as far as I was aware; and that I had mentioned it to none but Canon LIDDON and himself; that this reticence on my part was not that it may be kept to ourselves; but, *chiefly, that it might appear, and should in truth be, a spontaneous offering on the part of the authorities of St. Paul's, and proceeding from their own good and free will; and it appeared to me that in any case — as the offering must be unquestionably voluntary — no notice should be given officially, indeed none at all, to any of the American ecclesiastic authorities; for every appearance of previous understanding should be most carefully guarded against.*[1]

[1] And see the Memoir, Appendix, pp. 42, 44.

Dean CHURCH finally answered that he saw the importance of the opportunity, and agreed with me that the commemoration should be an event to be originated by the official authorities of the Cathedral, to go forth as "a free-will offering," and, he added good-humoredly, "as you have said, in expiation." Dean CHURCH recurs, perhaps, to this expression of mine, when in his letter of November 15 (the day after the commemorative service) he wrote to me: "The Archbishop preached a striking sermon, bolder and more frank in its tone than we have heard recently from Archbishops, a reparation for the weakness and stagnancy of 1784."[1]

It was thus decided that the Commemorative Service should be undertaken.

The Dean asked me if I had thought about a programme. I had: and this led us to consider particulars, wherein I did not withhold what had occurred to me. I mentioned some things that found place in the programme as after settled; which makes it clearer why the Reverend WILLIAM JONES SEABURY, D. D., who was the gospeller (a remarkable feature in the service), says to me, in his letter from London, written the day after the commemoration: "Only a line in the few minutes before the mail closes to tell you that your programme at St. Paul's was completely carried out and most successfully."[2]

[1] Appendix, p. 57.   [2] Appendix, pp. 58, 59.

I now perceived I might go farther, and—following up this advantageous opening—said that the fundamental merit of the recognition of the occasion by the Cathedral authorities would be more ample, adequate, and as if it were "reënforced," if the Archbishop of Canterbury took part personally, and officially on behalf of the Church of England itself. I then told him that Canon LIDDON had requested me to write a full memoir of the subject: a request from which we might conclude that the Canon would be willing to preach the sermon. But I suggested that it was demanded by the purpose and meaning and reach of the commemoration that the Archbishop should do it; that "that capstone would perfect the celebration as a monumental event, and confirm it by the highest ecclesiastical authority of Great Britain." The Dean promised to think over this: which he called a most valuable thought. He said that if he should judge it prudent and feasible to attempt, he would call on me the day but one following, at the hotel where I was staying. He called; I was away; and he left his card. I was, therefore, by this intimation, at liberty to assume that the Dean engaged to see the Archbishop.

If the Archbishop consented, then a change in our plan might become due and appropriate. This would deny us the happiness of Canon LIDDON being the preacher; but, however this might be, His Grace's presence was ardently to be desired:

for it was the requirement essential to a historical reparation by the Church of England, and to the highest ecclesiastical authoritative sanction of the commemoration. It was natural to presuppose that many would desire and expect a great discourse, on the great theme, from him whom they regarded the greatest pulpit orator of our time. The absence of LIDDON from the pulpit of St. Paul's on that occasion must be noted: yet, as the commemoration demanded, so it would have graciously and abundantly bestowed upon it, that sanction which was essential to its perfect signification. Certainly it was not an opportunity to gratify individual likings and wishes — to attain the object for which we set out and to fully accomplish its purposes were the things desired. So, when His Grace consented, with characteristic kindness and readiness, not only to confer upon the commemoration his official presence but to emphasize that act by preaching, it was esteemed, by those to whom in America and in England it was made known, a great boon; and it was, within the peculiar circumstances of the occasion, surely a most gracious act — nobly undertaken, and candidly and magnanimously performed, by the Archbishop. I was then of the opinion, since deepened into profound conviction, that the presence and the sermon of the Archbishop constituted the commanding and consummating incident of the day celebrated: truly, in the language of Dean CHURCH, "a reparation for the weakness and stagnancy of 1784."

It would be an unpardonable omission to leave unnoticed and unacknowledged the part which Canon LIDDON did bear to the event. He was, as I have already said, the first to whom I suggested the thought of having a commemoration at St. Paul's. Had November been one of the months during which he was to be in residence at the Cathedral, his own activity would have been more apparent and greater in the affair. He was the first to understand and to esteem its justice and importance: and to the end he was diligent wherever he could aid its promotion.[1]

LIDDON's heart was touched and pierced by the occasion, and was full of the spirit of the theme; and this I soon after could see more fully, and understand, from a letter he wrote me from Highclerc Castle, on November 28, 1884: "The general impression here was that the occasion was one for serious thankfulness to God. The pervading spirit was excellent, and the Archbishop's sermon in harmony with it, generally speaking; although I wish he had been able to state briefly, but firmly, the nature and necessity of the truth which was the inspiring nature of Bishop SEABURY's courageous

---

[1] It is not to be supposed — indeed it was not possible — that what I here relate of Canon LIDDON became known to the Archbishop. It was wholly private between the Canon and me — and, as to the supposition, at that time, that he might be induced to preach the sermon, it was simply an inference of my own, and as such mentioned to Dean CHURCH. Indeed, what I have said on the preceding page has indicated this.

act. He took it for granted; but, in view of the great ignorance of the mass of the people on religious subjects, something more explicit would have been welcome. I almost fear that it may seem ungrateful to His Grace to write in this way; but I wish to be perfectly honest when writing to you."[1]

Having accomplished my "heart's desire" I turned my way homeward. At Shrewsbury, where I rested for a few days before leaving for New York, I received a letter, dated at St. Andrew's, Scotland, July 29, 1884, from the venerable CHARLES WORDSWORTH, the Bishop of St. Andrews, an acquaintance and correspondent of mine.[2] It related to the com-

[1] Appendix, p. 59.

[2] The above was written before his death, and it appears to me that I should now add — what is due to his memory and intended for "a token of high respect and gratitude sincere" — an acknowledgment of the Bishop's efficient service promoting the Commemoration at Aberdeen. I was from the first made aware of his efforts. He was in whole accord with the spirit of the centennial celebration in Scotland; but the significance and value of the "reparation" offered to both the Churches of Scotland and America by the Church of England at St. Paul's was that which was most esteemed and most cherished by him as a member of the Church *of* (not merely *in*) Scotland.

CHARLES WORDSWORTH, D. D., D. C. L., Bishop of St. Andrews and Fellow of Winchester College, was born at Lambeth, England, on August 22, 1806. He was eminent as a scholar, in erudition and in classical learning, excelling in Latin versification, — he was the private tutor at Oxford of Gladstone, — famous in his Mastership at Winchester College, an author of acknowledged ability, and a preacher of high repute, yet it is probable that he will be more widely remembered and distinguished by his work on *Shakespeare's Knowledge and Uses of the Bible*. On Sunday, April 24, 1864, at Stratford-on-Avon, he was the sermoner at the Shakespeare Tercentenary Celebration. Our correspondence for some years related chiefly to his labors making

memoration festival to be held in October at Aberdeen. He wrote: "I only regret that your engagements require you to return home without paying us a visit in this country. When I first recognized your handwriting, and saw that it was dated from Shrewsbury, I was in hopes that you had come over for the centenary, where your presence would be so very appropriate and so highly welcome."[1] But I could not remain. I had work at home for the St. Paul's Commemoration.

Soon after my arrival at home I wrote (August 20, 1884) to Dean CHURCH, and gave him an additional hint for the programme, pointing out to him the felicitous propriety of the Reverend Dr. SEABURY, of New York, being invited to read the Gospel;[2] clear the pervading influence of the Tyndal and the standard English translations of the Bible on Shakespeare's mind, and literary taste, and skill. In the last letter but one which (dated Kilrymont, December 12, 1890) I received from the Bishop, he, recurring to this subject, his favorite occupation in latter years, says to me: "I have much pleasure in sending a photograph taken of me in Edinburgh only a fortnight ago. I am now in my eighty-fifth year.... My 'Shakespeare and the Bible' is now nearly out of print; and I am thinking of preparing a new edition.... I venture to ask whether you can give me any assistance for its improvement. Have you got the last (*third*) edition, which contains my Stratford Tercentenary Sermon, and other considerable additions? Those additions, entitled 'Additional Illustrations,' and now placed in an Appendix, I should wish to have inserted in their proper places of the main text."

The Bishop had forgotten that, at the time (1880) when the third edition was published, he sent to me a copy; and with kind words prefaced by his own hand opposite its title-page. His last gift to me was his *Discourses on the Primary Witness to the Truth of the Gospel* — his last publication.

[1] Appendix, p. 39.   [2] *Ibid.*, p. 41.

and I enclosed the promised "Memoir," in duplicate, — one for himself, the other, if required, for the Archbishop. Dr. SEABURY was not aware of this suggestion.[1] I posted to Canon LIDDON two copies of the memoir:[2] he to give one to Canon GREGORY. It was a lengthy paper of sixteen closely written pages. It furnished all biographical facts and incidents of SEABURY, and indulged in observations and reflections; some of which appear to have been worked into the Archbishop's sermon.[3]

Some remarks connected with Unitarianism in New England[4] and a curious incident attending its meeting-house at Hartford, related by me in that "Memoir," have, I am informed, not agreed with the understanding of certain persons, — one an eminent American prelate. I know nothing of my own knowledge of what I related; but hearsay was never sustained by better testimony, for all that I made use of came from the Honorable JAMES DIXON,

[1] Here I think it in place to quote from that letter: "I hesitate to make any suggestion as to details of the ceremonies — but it might be a pleasing and notable feature that the Rev. William Jones Seabury, D. D., the Bishop's great-grandson, should read the gospel for the day — in the very place from whence his noble ancestor was sent forth to preach the Gospel in America. Dr. Seabury will be in London within a few days after the celebration at Aberdeen; and I avail myself of your [general] permission and give him a letter to you. I have not, of course, mentioned anything of my suggestion as to his reading the gospel. You will be pleased with him; he is a learned, able, and unaffected man."

[2] Appendix, p. 40.
[3] *Ibid.*, pp. 70, 71. See note *a* to the Archbishop's sermon, *ibid.*, p. 70.
[4] *Ibid.*, p. 44.

of Hartford, a Senator of the United States, and who was a most active member of Trinity while it was yet of the Unitarian association. After he became a Churchman Mr. DIXON supervised the dilapidation of the old edifice. The ancient materials were at once moved to another part of the town; and there, each stone replaced in its former relation, the reconstructed edifice was consecrated by Bishop WILLIAMS, the Primate of our American Church; and the sermon was preached by Dr. HUNTINGTON, now the Bishop of Central New York, and who, when a preacher in Unitarianism, had himself often preached to gatherings within its walls. While on a visit to Mr. DIXON, in August, 1865, we viewed the "old materials," reërected and consecrated in the new site; and there he told me the story which I relate in the " Memoir."

The next stage, in order of time, was that, in the latter part of September, from Dean CHURCH, a letter came, dated the 17th, telling me: "We hope to have a Commemoration Service at St. Paul's on November 14; and, further, that the Archbishop of Canterbury has gladly consented to preach on the occasion. I enclose his note. Thank you for the paper which you were so good as to send me, and of which I sent one copy to the Archbishop."[1]

The time was now ripe when I might disclose what was done, and doing, to the Right Reverend HORATIO POTTER, Bishop of New York, and to the

[1] Appendix, p. 51.

Assistant Bishop, the Right Reverend HENRY COD-
MAN POTTER. The Assistant Bishop, answering
from Newport a note of mine, appointed Friday,
October 3d, to meet me in New York.[1] We met,
and I told him all without reserve; and showed
him Dean CHURCH'S letter of September 17. The
Assistant Bishop desired to acquaint the public
with the intelligence, and he requested me to write
to the Bishop. In compliance I sent a letter to
the Right Reverend HORATIO POTTER.[2]

The letter was published by the Bishop, and
with my consent, in the newspapers, and so the affair
became public. *It will be seen that I was careful to
have it made clear that the St. Paul's Commemoration Service was wholly a voluntary act, and that no
official notice to our Church was to be expected.*

Another letter came from Dean CHURCH, dated
"London, The Deanery, St. Paul's, Nov. 4, 1884,"
telling me: "All is settled for November 14. I
hoped to have sent you with my letter a copy of
the Service, but it is not ready for the printer. I
send you the Special Psalms, Lessons, and Collects,
all of Dr. LIDDON'S selection. As I told you, the
Archbishop will preach. . . . I have asked Dr.
SEABURY to read the Gospel. . . . I hope you will
accept it as an evidence of our sympathy, and
of the great and happy changes which a hundred
years have wrought in the ideas and feelings of
Churchmen on both sides of the water, and not

---

[1] Appendix, p. 52.   [2] *Ibid.*, pp. 52-53.

of Churchmen only, but of the two peoples who speak the English tongue. You will remember us on the 14th."¹

Canon LIDDON's original memoranda² of the "Special Psalms, Lessons, and Collects" were enclosed in that letter, and are among the "inset" papers, as, also, the note of the Archbishop,³ enclosed in the Dean's former letter.

There ended my part.

Afterwards I received from Canon LIDDON the letter written at Highclerc, from which I have quoted, and a letter from Dean CHURCH, written at the Deanery the day next after the Commemoration. The great event was consummated in the Cathedral, and at the time appointed. It is to the latter letter that attention is required. After fully describing, in glowing phrases and in minuteness, the entire ceremony and its incidents, the Dean says: "I tell you this, because you are the one person to whom the idea of this Commemoration, which many of us look at as a historical event, is entirely due."⁴ While this statement is probably wholly correct, it seemed strange at the time that the Dean should mention to me a fact known to each of us; yet I felt quite sure that he could not mean to offer a certificate of the part which I had borne to the event. My heart was satisfied that the event

[1] Appendix, p. 56. [2] *Ibid.*, p. 57.
[3] *Ibid.*, p. 52.   [4] *Ibid.*, p. 58.

was brought forth and the purpose accomplished. I had no wish further to be gratified. The circumstance passed from my mind, until it was revived by an incident, in the summer of 1888, when I visited again Dean CHURCH at the Deanery.

Since the Commemoration I have met and received kind attentions from those in England — except the manly and gentle LIDDON — who were concerned in it. Two of the three who then privately acted together in its initiation have passed "through nature to eternity." The occasion and the time are now come when I, the survivor of those three, am in duty bound to tell the tale. Wherefore I have caused to be "inset" the "original correspondence and other proof of that historical event" in a unique book, durably and appropriately bound: where they may hereafter be seen by those interested; and to which book I have, in my own penmanship, prefixed an introduction, the substance of which is contained in this memoir. The volume contains the original records of the whole course of proceeding. I shall finally lodge that book in a public place for safe care, and there accessible as material for history.

During our talk in 1888, Dean CHURCH called my attention to the printed "Form of Service" used at the ceremonies, and which was distributed to the congregation at the Commemoration. It had on its cover the words that the celebration was "*at the* REQUEST *of the American Bishops repre-*

senting the Sixty-five Dioceses of the Church in the United States which have sprung of Seabury's line"!![1]
It appeared that, as a copy of the Form of Service had been sent to me at New York the day of the Commemoration, the Dean had assumed I must notice the statement, and felt it should be, to my understanding, offensive, as a misconception and an untruth. Hence the letter[2] written by the Dean the very next day after the celebration, and stating to me: —

"*I tell you this, because you are the one person to whom the idea of this Commemoration, which many of us look at as a historical event, is entirely due. When you proposed it to me in the summer, I had not thought of it;* and all that I did was to approach the Archbishop, who received the proposal with the most cordial sympathy, and put off another engagement to take his part in it. *I hope you will let me thank you as a benefactor to both our Churches.*

Yours gratefully and faithfully,
R. W. CHURCH."[3]

The Dean had been disturbed by what he thought an injustice done to me; and I perceived that he, supposing I would observe it, had so promptly written that letter to set himself aright. I told him I had not noticed it; but that the proper question was not about me, — it was about the misstatement itself, which gave a false front to the object which Canon LIDDON, he, and myself had in our purpose. The "Form of Service" had been prepared by

[1] Appendix, p. 61.   [2] *Ibid.*, p. 58.
[3] The italicizing in this page is mine.

the Dean and Canon LIDDON themselves, and in their own handwriting; that part done by the latter was sent at the time to me, without my asking, as were all the other original drafts, for souvenirs; and it is preserved by me, with those others, in the book of which I have spoken. Nothing, I was assured, was uttered by either of them as to any "request of American Bishops." Canon LIDDON himself, as I am informed, was equally annoyed. I felt certain that the Dean suspected, if he did not know, the personage who, superserviceably, caused those words to be so absurdly intruded. I did not wish to learn, — I did not inquire. The swing of eloquence by which the announcement ends, that the request is made by the Bishops "which have sprung of SEA-BURY's line," almost sufficiently indicates the author of this maladroit act.

It is proper and commendable, therefore, to correct a statement — so published as if officially authorized — which asserted publicly, and so absurdly in the face of the primal and controlling intention and all the circumstances of the event, that the Commemoration was, on the part of the Church of England, a compliance with "the *request of the Bishops*" of the "Church in the United States." And the truth is that, by the time the Commemoration became feasible, and while details for the Service were under consideration, the American Bishops had left for their several dioceses, and only three of them then in England were at

St. Paul's. "You shall hear more when details are arranged," the Dean wrote to me — "But everybody is still out of town."[1] By another letter (November 4) he says: "We hope to have all your Bishops who are now in England: Albany, Minnesota, and Fond du Lac;"[2] and again (November 15) he adds: "We had our Service yesterday. . . . There were *three* American Bishops — I wish we had more, but they were gone."[3] There is nothing in those letters about any request, nor about Bishops representing sixty-five or any less number of Dioceses! But, in verity and candor, such a statement, *if ever credited*, would be not only contradictory of the originating spirit, and of the scope and object of the St. Paul's "reparation," but would blur the aspect and deny the magnanimity of its coming to the Church in America a "free-will offering," — as, indeed, it did — unasked, unannounced, unexpected. Wherefore, in correction of any such perversion, I write and publish this Memoir. It was of this initiative purpose on the part of the official authority at St. Paul's I had written to Bishop HORATIO POTTER, after receiving the Dean's first letter. Dean CHURCH and Canon LIDDON felt this perversion of the intention and object which impelled us to produce the event; and they were anxious that the unhappy incident, if it should ever obtain currency, might not impair the efficacy of what Dean CHURCH calls "a reparation for the weakness and stagnancy of 1784." That

[1] Appendix, p. 51. [2] *Ibid.*, p. 56. [3] *Ibid.*, p. 57.

reparation was to be unsolicited: — That was alone the excuse why a layman should have made the suggestion. No one in ecclesiastical authority in the United States could make such a request, without incurring the censure of being a suppliant for a recognition which we know the SEABURY succession does not need: and which our dioceses would not permit to be questioned. Yet that is just what a well-meaning marplot, afflicted by an unappeasable desire to do good, has made appear. It was a blunder.

Where was the Church of Scotland in this Commemoration? She was surely interested, and, by the same invitation as that offered to the American Bishops, her Bishops were associated in its reparatory scope.[1] Her Bishops were present, they

---

[1] It is well to emphasize this comment, by here reflecting upon the Archbishop's appropriate, candid, and nervous statement of the case, which was then and there to be considered, of The Church of Scotland: " Once more in the Church's history God committed deliverance not to the strong but to the smallest and feeblest of all. The third person of the drama, the Church once 'of Scotland,' was in the dust. Her Officers and her Offices lay under terrible disabilities. Legislation had recently attempted to annihilate even what a writer of the times properly called 'her shattered remains.' She worshipped under penal statutes, the more insulting because no one would now have executed them. Still she could not emerge from back streets and upper floors. And the poor remnant of her Bishops, four in number, lived, driven into one diocese, in poverty and in piety. Her very existence was a breach of law, like that of a Church of the first days under a humane emperor. Her holiest acts were offences, the more sacred the more criminal. She was asked to undertake what The Church of England was not strong enough to effect. And thus she answered in the person

united in the great consummation, and they received there, on behalf of "the Catholic remainder of the antient Church of Scotland,"[1] the testimony of a redress due to more than a century and a half of unjust negation.

It has — ever since I learned of the eccentric deviation from the true history of the origin and object of the Commemoration — been my intention that, when the occasion and the time came, a full and corrected record should be made. This I now

of one of her poor prelates: 'Considering the great *depositum* committed to us, I do not see how we can account to our great Lord and Master if we neglect such an opportunity of promoting His truth and enlarging the borders of His Church.' So then, while the new States eyed Episcopacy with a suspicious hate that had its roots in the past, and believed it to be irreconcilable with the interests of a Republic, little knowing what strength it had lent to every form of government in its turn; while the idea of it seemed, alas! so lost in State-craft that even the Church of America itself partly doubted for a while whether its orders were certainly valid, as having been conferred without the consent of a State; while a proposal was being ventilated for a nominal Episcopacy created by lay and clerical votes; while our Lord Chancellor was instructing the House of Lords that the Episcopal clergy for other countries should be ordained by English and Irish prelates only — while such were the 'counsels of princes,' the feeble remnant in Scotland was quietly facing the crisis of the Church of the future. Humbly and peacefully, with knowledge of what they were doing, they laid their hands on the chosen man in an upper chamber, and imparted to the New World the gift of 'a free, valid and purely ecclesiastical Episcopacy.' These were their own words, 'free, valid, and purely ecclesiastical.' It is no wonder that those ringing words sound again and again in the letters of that time, and that they were incorporated in the 'beloved concordat' which ruled the relations of Scotland and America."

[1] Appendix, see Concordat, p. 86: on that page.

perform: — the occasion, when I have gathered together, in a form appropriate and well-chosen for preservation, the original manuscripts, which of themselves tell the story; the time, when RICHARD WILLIAM CHURCH[1] and HENRY PARRY LIDDON,[2] my consociates in the affair, are taken from this life.

As I pen its last lines, I feel as is expressed in the closing words of the Second Book of the Maccabees: "And if I have done well, and as is fitting the story, it is that which I desired; but if slenderly and meanly, it is that which I could attain unto." I have no pride of place myself, nor feeling of elation. Whatever sentiment I have ever been conscious of has always been that of humility and thankfulness. In the hands of Providence the weakest are fully efficient.

GEO: SHEA.

NEW YORK, 205 WEST 46TH STREET,
   Feast of The Annunciation, 1893.

[1] Died, December 15, 1890.   [2] Died, September 9, 1890.

Nulla Ecclesia Sine Episcopo
SEABURY'S MOTTO

Appendices:

CORRESPONDENCE AND OTHER PROOF OF THE COMMEMORATION

Appendices

Page ante 22.

BISHOPSHALL, ST. ANDREWS, July 29, '84.

MY DEAR SIR, — I thank you very much for your kind and interesting letter, and for the trouble you have been so good as to take. I only regret that your engagements require you to return home without paying us a visit in this country. When I first recognized your handwriting and saw that you dated from Shrewsbury, I was in hopes that you had come over for the Centenary; where your presence would be so very appropriate, and so highly welcome. It is some consolation however to think that by returning you may be able to persuade Dr. Seabury to accept the Bishop of Aberdeen's invitation.

I ought to have written before to thank you for your communication of last September which I was glad to receive and have kept by me. It is not probable that I shall live to see another edition of my "Shakespeare and the Bible," as I shall enter next month upon my 78th year; but I do not forget your kind interest in the book, and should much value any contribution which you may at any time send me for its improvement. I am anxious to get it introduced *as a prize book into schools* for which I venture to think it is not unsuitable upon more than one account.

I am, my dear sir,
Yours very faithfully,
C. WORDSWORTH.

Page 23.

Personal. NEW YORK, Aug. 20th, 1884.

VERY REV. AND DEAR DEAN, — Since my arrival, some twelve days ago, I have had urgent demands on my time which delayed the "discourse" that I enclose. I did not like to recite all the reasons which I gave to you in conversation: but I assure you that we cannot overestimate the benefits that are likely to spring from such a celebration of the Centenary as St. Paul's alone can undertake and present.

I enclose my letter in duplicate; as, should you lay the affair before His Grace of Canterbury in pursuance of your thought to have him preach the sermon, you might deem it desirable to leave one of the duplicates with the Archbishop. I send a similar letter to Canon Liddon according to his permission: for his own use, and to be used, perhaps in unison with you, in an interview with Canon Gregory. I hope and expect that Canon Gregory will take kindly and warmly to the suggestion, when either Canon Liddon or yourself present it. Several of our own bishops and distinguished of our clergy have accepted the invitation of the Primate and other Scotch bishops to be present at their celebration for the 5th, 6th, 7th, and 8th October. But no celebration can reach the moral value of the proposed ceremony on the exact day of consecration — Nov. 14 — in St. Paul's. From that mother-church went forth the missionaries of the Society for the Propagation of the Gospel in America, whose labors cleared the field for the establishment of the Episcopate here: from that spot Bishop Sherlock (Dec. 1753) sent forth the priest Seabury, who was to be, in the fullness of time, the first bishop. You will notice that Seabury had his degree of doctor conferred on him by Oxford.

I hesitate to make any suggestion as to details of the ceremonies — but it might be a pleasing and notable feature that the Rev. William Jones Seabury, D. D., the Bishop's great-grandson, should read the gospel for the day — in the very place from whence his noble ancestor was sent forth to preach the Gospel in America. Dr. Seabury will be in London within a few days after the celebration at Aberdeen; and I avail myself of your permission and give him a letter to you. I have not, of course, mentioned anything of my suggestion as to his reading the gospel. You will be pleased with him; he is a learned, able, and unaffected man.

Ever faithfully,
GEO. SHEA.

To the Very Rev. DEAN CHURCH.

Pages 23, 24.

NEW YORK, Aug. 19th, '84.
7 Nassau Street.

VERY REVEREND AND DEAR DEAN, — I avail myself of the privilege which you have opened; and address you concerning the anniversary of the establishment of The Church in America. A hundred years nearly have passed since that great epoch in our Church began in the consecration of Samuel Seabury at Longeau, Aberdeen, Scotland, on November 14, 1784, by Bishop Kilgour, *primus;*

Bishop Petrie, and Bishop Skinner, who described themselves in the Concordat,[1] then made with this newly-created American Bishop, as " of the Catholic remainder of the ancient Church." There appears to have been significant and historical truth in that description, as a table[2] of their Episcopal succession, now before me, attests.

It seems to those of our faith in America that such an event should be thankfully and piously celebrated; and directions have been authoritatively given to that end. At the Convention last autumn I had the honor to be appointed one of the lay members of the Committee who are to suggest a form of celebration proper for this Diocese. Though not within the scope of the duties of that Committee — still, as a personal suggestion, induced by the friendly regard with which you have often honored me, I venture to offer a suggestion which, it seems to me, this superb occasion warrants; and which the manifest benefits likely to arise from its adoption might commend to the wisdom and brotherly love of those high and highest in our mother Church of England.

It would be an assumption for those in the American Church to make a request; but it has occurred to me, as I have personally stated to you, that perhaps a churchman like myself not in official ecclesiastical authority might suggest to you, as the Dean of St. Paul's, how gracious and becoming would be *a voluntary recognition* of this Centenary by a special service in St. Paul's Cathedral — that Cathedral to which American churchmen are taught to look, and always look up to, as our Metropolitan, and as the

[1] See *infra*, pp. 85–89.   [2] See *infra*, between pp. 84, 85.

Appendices

Propaganda of those churches which have proceeded from the Anglican successions.

The Church in Scotland has already determined, — and this comes of its own unprompted wish, — to mark the event by solemn services, and it has completed its arrangements for the 5th – 8th October next. This somewhat anticipates, you will perceive, the actual day of Dr. Seabury's consecration; the reason for which is that those Bishops and Clergy invited from the American States might return in time for their duties at home. Among those specially invited by the Scottish Bishops to take part in those services is the Rev. William Jones Seabury, D. D., the great-grandson and nearest living lineal descendant of the Bishop. He is the Rector of the Church of The Annunciation in New York, and the Professor of Ecclesiastical Polity and Law in our Theological College in this city. Bishops and other ecclesiastical personages are also invited to be present at the ceremonies from The Church of England.

The celebration by The Church of Scotland will be significantly commemorative and one of which we shall be proud. But it cannot attain for us, nor hold, that "vantage ground" which, historically and in our veneration, belongs, in this view, to The Church of England. From the Society for the Propagation of the Faith, under authority and license of The Church of England, came to the American Colonies those missionaries who, in these new fields, first met and checked the politico-religious intolerance of the Puritan. This was before the States became independent of and separate from the British Crown. The history of those days should be written — there is no prouder and fewer fruitful chapters in the history of the missionary labors and triumphs of the Anglican Church. The State of Connecticut — the diocese to which Seabury was elected and for which he was consecrated; the home of Jonathan Edwards, and then and long afterwards the hotbed[1] of Unitarianism — is this day throughout its land without a house of Unitarian worship. The last house for such worship has years ago been consecrated in the service of our Faith. Its last Unitarian minister is now the Bishop of Central New York, Dr. Huntington.

Is it not proper, "sweet and commendable," an obligation which the Metropolitan Cathedral of the Anglican World owes to its own position as our ancient centre and propaganda, to confirm the results of its own missionary success in America, and our growing filial sympathies, by a special service acknowledging the event of not merely the establishment, but of the grateful acceptance of the Episcopal order and The Church in a land that was once the peculiar domain of the Puritan. Such an act, *springing from the willing kindness of those in authority, as yourself*, would do more to bind closer and firmer, as "in hoops of steel," Anglican and American Churchmen than can be estimated in cool words; though it may be haply guessed.

Some facts and thoughts are appropriate herein as to the man in whose person this church work was begun, and by the abiding spirit of whose intrepid

---

[1] It may be that the phrase used here is somewhat exaggerated: but surely the substance of the thought is appropriate; for, if that region was not a hotbed of Unitarianism, surely that moral philosophy always found a welcome there, and a warm, hospitable corner at its hearths.

Appendices

discretion and uncompromising charity, our American Church has steadily gained unto its present almost national standing and authority throughout this Empire of States.

Samuel Seabury was born November 30, 1729, at Groton, near New London, in the Colony of Connecticut; he was educated at and graduated from Yale College, in New Haven, that State, 1748; he afterwards went to Edinburgh, Scotland, and studied medicine at the University, but, after acquiring a very competent knowledge in that science, he elected to devote himself to the study of theology, and with proper preparation he was ordained deacon on Friday, December 21, 1753, and on the Sunday following, admitted to priest orders, and on the same day, by Sherlock, Bishop of London, licensed and authorized to perform the office of priest in New Jersey, and in 1754 he entered upon his duties at New Brunswick, in that Province. He was, on January 12, 1757, collated and inducted into the parish of Jamaica, Long Island, by Sir Charles Hardy, Governor of New York; and having been instituted rector of St. Peter's, in Westchester County, by mandate of Sir Henry Moore, December 3, 1766, he was formally inducted to that office March 1, 1767, by the Rev. Myles Cooper, D. D., President of King's College, in the city of New York.

The Clergy of the Church of England, Missionaries in the Province of New York, felt a special interest in the controversy in which that Church was the chief and direct object of political attack. The famous William Livingston — who inherited the bias of his ancestor Robert Livingston, the non-conformist divine who settled at Rotterdam,

Holland, after he had been one of the Commissioners in 1650 to Charles II. at Breda — was publishing a party-organ, "The American Whig," in New York, and conducting the fierce memorable opposition made to any project to establish an episcopate in America by the Church of England. His party was numerically great and overwhelming. The strife between the Church in America and those who clustered about the various bodies of Dissenters was one of long continuance. It began as early as 1753 (the year before Seabury came as priest to America), and, though its heat had abated, it was prepared to break out afresh at any moment. It was most fierce and unqualified by charity in Massachusetts; but less fierce in New York only by comparison. Therefore, in the triumph of a revolt for political independence and separation, nothing less was feared than absolute and utter prostration for the Church; and while the Clergy wished well to the King, they desired better for the Church. Seabury was the main and most powerful antagonist of this anti-episcopate party; a powerful and prolific writer. He was a stout churchman, of strong convictions, and, by those convictions, a loyalist. He was sincerely and proudly an American, in the sense in which Bishop Berkeley and Benjamin Franklin were, when they each saw the greater future of the Colonies in a grander British Empire in America; but, like Berkeley, Seabury wished to see the Church, in its Episcopal authority, able to accompany, independently, the State in the boundless sphere of missionary duty which arose before their imaginations.

In simple, earnest words, written by him in the

hour of exile and affliction, in 1783, at London, he tells the story of that period. His dread of the influence which the Puritan minds of Massachusetts were directing against the introduction of the Church into New England, was equal almost to the hatred which Massachusetts professed against the Episcopate. He feared, likewise, the concerted plans to a similar end which were still kept in operation by William Livingston and his coherents. Those were of that kind which was most active in propagating doctrines going to alienate the hearts of the colonists from and to uproot the few and slender plants which the Anglican Church had lodged in the new world. Seabury fully apprehended the course which probable events would take. "Some years after," he himself relates, "when it was evident from continued publications in newspapers, and from the uniting of all the jarring interests of the Independents and Presbyterians from Massachusetts to Georgia, under grand Committees and Synods, that some mischievous scheme was meditated against the Church of England . . . in America," he entered "into an agreement with the Rev. Dr. T. B. Chandler, then of Elizabethtown, New Jersey, and the Rev. Dr. Inglis, the Rector of Trinity Church in the city of New York, to watch all publications, either in newspapers or in pamphlets, and so obviate the evil influence of such as appear to have a bad tendency, by the speediest answers." Faithfully and assiduously Seabury did his part of the agreement — he and his two associates bore the whole weight of the polemic controversy. In November, 1775, a body of men, to whom the writings of Seabury were objectionable, set out from New Haven,

Connecticut, for the purpose of seizing the persons of Seabury, Lord Underhill, the Mayor of the Borough of Westchester, and a Mr. Fowler, one of the Justices of the County. On their way they were joined by some eighty others going to New York; after burning a small sloop at Mamaroneck, and taking Underhill and Fowler, the party went (November 19) to the rectory of Seabury, and "not finding him at home (*Seabury MSS.*) they beat his children to oblige them to tell where their father was; which not succeeding, they searched the neighborhood and took him from his school," and placed him under a strong guard to be conducted to Connecticut. The guard, "with much abusive language," proceeded with the prisoner "in great triumph to New Haven, seventy miles distant, where he was paraded through most of the streets, and their success celebrated by firing of cannon," etc. At New Haven he was confined under a military guard and keepers for six weeks. When released, and after his return to his rectory, he suffered much, both from insult and the loss of property, by parties who were almost daily passing through his parish to join the recruits for the army then beginning to gather in New York. His home, during his absence, was pillaged, and he with his family left destitute. In June, 1777, he was appointed by Sir William Howe, Chaplain to the Provincial Hospital at New York; and in January, 1778, Chaplain to the King's American Regiment. He held those offices till he went from New York, on the 7th of June, 1783, direct to England, and there he, in lodgings at No. 393 Oxford Street, London, resolutely and hopefully meditated how best to serve the

Appendices

Church, which was nearest and ever in his heart of hearts. Seabury had done what he believed to be his duty to the King and to the State — that had passed. His God and the Church remained. To America he had determined to return, and there resume the labor of his Master's vineyard. He was disenthralled from a conscientious, but embarrassing, allegiance. Providence had permitted his native land to be a state without a King; it was his cherished task to see that his native land should have a Church, and not without a Bishop. *Nulla ecclesia sine episcopo* was the legend which he adopted to proclaim his design. That is still to this day the legend, inscribed beneath a bishop's mitre, upon the organ of the Church of The Annunciation, in New York city: the Church founded by his grandson. Seabury saw that his true mission and purpose of life now opened to him. He was elected in Connecticut to be its Bishop. He applied to one or more of the English Bishops for consecration; they, for some passing political reason, delayed; so, greatly as he preferred that his episcopal authority and apostolic power should proceed from the Church of England, by which he had been ordained deacon and priest, he applied to the Church of Scotland, and was sent to be the first bishop of the American Church. On the Sunday after his arrival, June 20, 1785, he preached his first sermon in America at Newport, at which place he landed; it was delivered from the pulpit where Berkeley had often proclaimed aspirations that the Church might be "planted" in America. And it is worthy of reflection to note that Seabury fixed the seat of his Episcopal See in that very Connecticut to which he had been led a prisoner by violent men, paraded a captive through the streets of its chief city, and immured in its jail for six weeks, insulted and threatened.

But he came there to preach a greater peace than that which had resulted from the shock of arms. He was at last heard and respected by those who had dreaded the Church and his office. His great sufferings in the cause of The Faith had won their admiration and confidence. He was to them still the same simple, grand, conciliatory, uncompromising man. He was careful to omit nothing that the sacerdotal traditions of time and custom had associated with his high office. In his office he buried his personality, and subscribed himself "Samuel of Connecticut," and a mitre, still preserved "with religious care" in our Trinity College, at Hartford, Connecticut, pressed his brows. In his private life he was most frugal and unostentatious. His sermons, in their style, remind us of those which Sherlock spoke when Master of the Temple. Perhaps there is a reason why Sherlock's writings had so much influence upon Samuel Seabury, for, besides receiving ordination under the supervision of that prelate, "Episcopacy, or the patriarchate" in America, was said to have been first proposed by Sherlock in the reign of George II.

The University of Oxford had conferred upon Seabury the degree of Doctor of Sacred Theology, December 15, 1777.

He died suddenly February 25, 1796, in the 67th year of his age. His bodily remains are buried in the crypt, beneath St. James' Church, New London, in the State of Connecticut: honored by the reverence of that diocese of which he was the first

Bishop, and by a people who have learned to esteem and respect him as citizen and prelate.

Somewhat at a hazard of delivering a "discourse," I have taxed your attention maybe more than your kindness meant to incur: but, feeling the importance of the occasion to the English and American Church, I have not hesitated to exceed rather than fall short of what could be expected: and once again, thanking you for the permission on which I have written to you,

    I am, my dear Dean Church,
        With great esteem and respect,
            Yours faithfully,
                GEO. SHEA.

To the Very Rev. R. W. CHURCH, D. D.,
Dean of St. Paul's, London.

Page 30.

THE DEANERY, ST. PAUL'S, September 17, 1884.

MY DEAR MR. JUSTICE SHEA, — I have waited to acknowledge your letter till I could tell you something about the subject of it. I am able now to tell you that we hope to have a Commemoration Service at St. Paul's on November 14; and, further, that the Archbishop of Canterbury has gladly consented to preach on the occasion. I enclose his note.

You shall hear more when details are arranged; but everybody is still out of town.

Thank you for the paper which you were so good as to send me, and of which I sent one copy to the Archbishop.

        Yours very faithfully,
           R. W. CHURCH.

(Enclosed in above letter.)

ADDINGTON PARK, CROYDON, September 12, 1884.

MY DEAR MR. DEAN, — The 14th of November was engaged, but I felt that I must not say no to such a request of yours. I will therefore, God willing, preach on anniversary of Seabury's consecration.

I heartily trust that you are better for your holiday, and that Mrs. Church and you all are well.

Ever affectionately yours,
EDW. CANTUAR.

Page 25.

NEWPORT, R. I., September 30, 1884.

MY DEAR JUDGE SHEA, — Your note has just reached me here, and I shall be at your service on Friday, October 3d, between 11 A. M. and 1 P. M., at 96 Fourth Ave., New York.

Very respectfully yours,
H. C. POTTER.

Page 25.

NEW YORK, October 4, 1884.

RIGHT REV. AND DEAR SIR, — It is a happy satisfaction for me to communicate to you, that I have received a letter, dated September 17, 1884, from the Very Rev. R. W. Church, the Dean of St. Paul's, London, enclosing a note to him from His Grace the Archbishop of Canterbury, which inform me that, on November 14 next, the centennial anniversary of the consecration of the Rev. Samuel Seabury, it is purposed to celebrate by an appropriate special service in St. Paul's Cathedral that commanding event in the history of the Church. I enclose copies of those letters.

Appendices

You will notice — though from Dean Church's letter all the proceedings are not yet arranged — that the Archbishop himself will preach the anniversary sermon.

The proposed celebration is in recognition of the epoch in the Church which had its beginning in the fact of the consecration of Bishop Seabury as the first American Bishop. *It springs from an unforced and fraternal accord, and from those highest in veneration and authority in The Church of England. Perhaps no official communication of this intention may be expected by our side, and from what now seem to me obvious reasons. Indeed, I apprehend that the information of which I have spoken is sent to me entirely in a personal and informal spirit,* and because I have had, through friendly conversations with Dean Church and with Canon Liddon, some relation to those impulses which have secured proper notice in England to the approaching anniversary.

Therefore — as *no formal communication can be surely expected, owing to what may be thought proprieties peculiar to such voluntary homage,* and as it must be assumed that a thing so important and valuable to an American Churchman cannot be meant for me only — I infer it is my duty, even at the risk of being open to the charge of intruding my own name on so great an occasion, to call, in this manner, the attention of the Bishop of New York to that which has been written to me.

With much esteem and respect,
   I am, my dear Bishop,
    Yours most faithfully,
      GEO. SHEA.

To the Right Rev. HORATIO POTTER, D. D.,
Bishop of New York.

Page 25.

HOBART COLLEGE, GENEVA, October 16, 1884.

MY DEAR CHIEF JUSTICE SHEA, — Owing to my absence from home, I have been hindered from acknowledging your letter until now. I am greatly indebted to you for all that you send me, and shall take the liberty, in accordance with your kind permission, of giving your letter addressed to me to the press, so soon as I can arrange for some appropriate observance of November 14th in New York. My own idea is that it would be an admirable arrangement to have the service in old Trinity, and ask Dr. Dix to repeat the sermon he preached in Scotland. How does this strike you?

Once more let me thank you for your letter and the copy of your most interesting communication to the Dean of St. Paul's, which accompanied it; and believe me, my dear Mr. Chief Justice,

Very faithfully yours,
H. C. POTTER.

Pages 25, 26.

3 AMEN COURT, ST. PAUL'S, E. C., October 7, 1884.

DEAR MR. JUSTICE SHEA, — Of your two very welcome letters, the earlier and longer reached me in Munich. The second awaits me on my return home.

The Dean of St. Paul's will, I hope, take some measures for carrying out your wishes in November. I fear that I may, too, probably miss Dr. Seabury, as I am obliged to go into Gloucestershire and then to Oxford, almost immediately. But I hope that this may not be so.

With our kindest regards to Mrs. Shea, pray believe me,

Always yours most truly,
H. P. LIDDON.

Mr. Justice SHEA.

Page 25.

NEW YORK, October 31, 1884.

VERY REV. AND DEAR DEAN CHURCH, — Yours of the 17th of last month, enclosing the note from His Grace the Archbishop of Canterbury, came in course to me. Soon after I called personally on the Bishop of New York and on the Assistant Bishop, with each of whom I have the happiness to be in friendly intercourse; and, entirely unofficially of course, communicated to them the intelligence that you purposed to have such a special service in St. Paul's on the centennial, and that the Archbishop had consented to preach an anniversary sermon. It has effected a profound and grateful impression with us, and the international results for our common good as Churchmen are likely to exceed even our sanguine anticipations.

Our own special service for the occasion will be held at our old Trinity, in this city; and the Bishop of Connecticut (Dr. Williams) will preach the anniversary sermon. He is just back from the centenary festival held at Aberdeen.

I await with pleasing expectation the order of proceedings for the service at St. Paul's, which order you so kindly promise to send to me.

On the day of the anniversary it is likely you will

receive from us a cable message appropriate to the time.

With great esteem and respect,
Yours very faithfully,
GEO. SHEA.

To the Very Rev. Dean CHURCH, D. D.

Pages 26, 30.

THE DEANERY, ST. PAUL'S, November 4, 1884.

MY DEAR JUDGE SHEA, — I write a line, before I leave home for a few days, to tell you that all is settled for November 14. I hoped to have sent you with my letter a copy of the Service, but it is not ready for the printer. I send you the Special Psalms, Lessons, and Collects, all of Dr. Liddon's selection. As I told you, the Archbishop will preach. We hope to have all your Bishops who are now in England: Albany, Minnesota, and Fond du Lac. I hope also that four if not five of the Scotch Bishops will take part — Aberdeen, Argyle, Breslin, and Edinburgh — the other three are incapacitated by bad health; and I hope we shall have a good muster of American churchmen. I have asked Dr. Seabury to read the Gospel. Of course there is the disadvantage of its being a supplementary commemoration, after the Aberdeen one. But I hope you will accept it as an evidence of our sympathy; and of the great and happy changes which a hundred years have wrought in the ideas and feeling of Churchmen on both sides of the water, and not of Churchmen only, but of the two peoples who speak the English tongue.

You will remember us on the 14th.

Yours very faithfully,
R. W. CHURCH.

Appendices

(*Canon Liddon's Selection, enclosed in above letter.*)

PROPER PSALMS. — Ps. 1, 127, 133, 147.
FIRST LESSON. — Deuteronomy xxix. 9–29.
SECOND LESSON. — Titus i. 5–9.
COLLECT (as in consecration of Bishops).
EPISTLE. — Acts xx. 17 (as in consecration of Bishops).
GOSPEL. — St. John xx. 19 (as in consecration of Bishops).

Pages 26, 30, 31.

THE DEANERY, ST. PAUL'S, November 15, 1884.

MY DEAR JUDGE SHEA, — We had our Service yesterday: I think it made an impression on all there, and it is commented on with much friendly sympathy by the "Times," which does not always show such honor to St. Paul's. I will send you the Form of Service, in which the Lessons and Psalms were chosen by Dr. Liddon. The Archbishop preached a striking sermon, bolder and more frank in its tone than we have heard recently from Archbishops — a reparation for the weakness and stagnancy of 1784. There was a long line of Bishops in the procession; American, Scotch, English, Colonial, mixed fraternally according to the order of their consecration; — they were seated in the Sacrarium; and the administration was by two English, London and Durham; two American, Minnesota and Albany; and two Scotch, Edinburgh and Glasgow. There were *three* American Bishops — I wish we had more, but they were gone — five Scotch, and the rest up to the number of twenty-eight (I believe), English and Colonial: among them, besides those I have mentioned, Ely, Oxford, Lichfield, Chichester, Rochester, Truro, St. Alban's, Moritzburg, Nassau. Dr. Seabury was gospeller, and read the Gospel. Fond du Lac made the third American Bishop. I invited the American Minister, and he came and sat in the choir, opposite to the Archbishop. Dr. Liddon was there. The Dome and Choir were quite full.

I tell you this, because you are the one person to whom the idea of this Commemoration, which many of us look at as a historical event, is entirely due. When you proposed it to me in the summer, I had not thought of it; and all that I did was to approach the Archbishop, who received the proposal with the most cordial sympathy, and put off another engagement to take his part in it. I hope you will let me thank you as a benefactor to both our Churches.

Yours gratefully and faithfully,
R. W. CHURCH.

Page 17.

LONDON, November 15, 1884.

DEAR JUDGE, — Only a line in the few minutes before the mail closes to tell you that your programme at St. Paul's was completely carried out and most successfully.

The Service was beyond everything I ever saw, and the Archbishop's sermon was equal to the occasion, and that is saying a good deal.

All of his sermon has mind and force, and showed mastery of his subject and of the history pertaining to it; but he evidently was enkindled with enthusiasm about Bishop Seabury. He quoted your words, remarking of Bishop Seabury: "'He has been well described as a simple, grand, conciliating, but uncompromising man,' and his portrait shows a face which indicates him to have been worthy of the double antithesis."

Appendices

Your friend Lord Truro has behaved most kindly to us. We dined with him last night. I spent last Sunday at Addington Park with the Archbishop very pleasantly; lots of talk I hope to have with you, if it please God to bring us home safely. Kind regards to Mrs. Shea and your children, and
        I am as ever,
                Yours affectionately,
                      W. J. SEABURY.
HON. GEORGE SHEA.

Pages 20, 21, 26.

HIGHCLERC CASTLE, November 28, 1884.

MY DEAR MR. JUSTICE SHEA, — I have been hoping to write to you ever since November 14th, but have been prevented by a variety of occupations and interruptions. By this time you will have heard, perhaps even from some who were present, an account of what took place. The general impression here was that the occasion was one for serious thankfulness to God. No doubt many details might have been better managed; but the pervading spirit was excellent, and the Archbishop's sermon in harmony with it, generally speaking; although I wish he had been able to state briefly, but firmly, the nature and necessity of the truth which was the inspiring motive of Bishop Seabury's courageous act. He took it for granted; but, in view of the great ignorance of the mass of people on religious subjects, something more explicit would have been welcome. I almost fear that it may seem ungrateful to His Grace to write in this way, *but I wish to be perfectly honest when writing to you.*

My only disappointment was that I missed seeing

Dr. Seabury, except in the distance. He called at my house when I was out of town; and I had to leave London again on the 14th, immediately after the service at St. Paul's. I had the satisfaction of hearing him read the Gospel in a clear, fine voice — an incident in the day's proceedings which commanded general interest.

This letter requires no reply whatever, and will conclude by my assuring you that I am,
Dear Mr. Justice Shea,
Yours most truly,
H. P. LIDDON.

Pray make my kind respects to Mrs. Shea and the Misses Shea.

NOVEMBER 14, 1884.

A SPECIAL SERVICE
OF
COMMEMORATION

Held in

ST. PAUL'S CATHEDRAL,

At the request of the American Bishops representing the Sixty-five Dioceses of the Church in the United States which have sprung of Seabury's line.

The Holy Communion
Celebrated at 11 a. m.

THE SERMON

Preached by HIS GRACE the

ARCHBISHOP OF CANTERBURY,

And the Offertory appropriated by the Dean and Chapter to

The Society for the Propagation of the Gospel in Foreign Parts.

The Sermon

PREACHED IN ST. PAUL'S

BY

THE ARCHBISHOP OF CANTERBURY.

"Deep calleth unto Deep."

"Let the Lord, the God of the spirits of all flesh, set a man over the congregation . . . that the congregation of the Lord be not as sheep which have no shepherd." — NUMBERS xxvii. 16, 17.

A WARRIOR-STATESMAN was the gift which the lawgiver prayed his God to give Israel. He besought Him as "God of the spirits of all flesh," because he knew how through the gift of a great man God touches man's spirit, wins the enthusiasm and the imagination and the firm resolve of multitudes to any enterprise He has in hand for them to execute. It was no warrior-prince of whom Christ was thinking when this text of the Old Testament recurred to His memory in all the pathos of its fulfilling. He too saw the multitudes and had compassion, yearned upon them, because they were "rent and tossed about"[1] as sheep that have no shepherd. What Moses dreaded for his people in the deserts, Christ found to be the case of His people amid their towns. And because He was God of the spirits of all flesh, He knew how

[1] ἐσκυλμένοι καὶ ἐρριμμένοι, St. Matt. ix. 36.

many hard hearts as well as broken hearts, how many seemingly proud spirits as well as contrite ones, needed in reality to be gathered and comforted. And so, we read, "He called to Him His disciples and gave them authority,"— gave them shepherds, and not warriors, spiritual men "to go out before them and to go in before them, and to lead them out, and to bring them in "— and " He gave them authority."

In general, it is strange to notice how the needs, sufferings, and aspirations of people, taken together in a mass, awaken little feeling, to speak of, in proportion to the interest we take in individuals. When multitudes are rich in power and prosperity, and the self-will of combination, then we think little of the individual. The man or the woman, with his losses or her wrongs, his failure or her shame, must be crushed by the relentless onward tramp. Then the multitude is everything. But when the multitude itself suffers from faulty legislation, or from its own habits formed under that baleful influence, how difficult it has been to get their weight of misery or darkness considered and planned for. The labor of thousands for wages that mock the work, the flinging of vilest temptations before them in heaps in their streets, the bestowal of relief in ways that make idleness a career, the ignorance and the idolatries of tribes and nations, are beheld without compassion enough to move any but the most self-denying to the rescue. And yet the sorrows of an individual, even his sentimental troubles, the agitations of his mind, will at the same moment have for us an absorbing interest. If by any personification we could only place before ourselves the Churches of America, England, Scotland, as they were a century ago and had then been for half a

Appendices

century, pleading, pausing, succoring, like three fair women distracted with anxiety, with inability, with forbidden sympathy, the tale of those times would leave few cheeks unwet. But because they were merely multitudes, countries, Churches, in which thousands of minds and hearts throbbed and worked, their hopes, fears, and aspirations compose but a commonplace page of history.

I wish to turn that old page, full of interest, romance, intense life, and yet no tale of sentiment. It is an action of men, honorable men of the world. There is firm urgency of just demands, a manly patience, and, one policy failing, the dignified adoption of another. There is unity of principle with the greatest change of mode. I am bidden to give expression to this, as a call to stronger sympathy, to more thankful faith, to harder-strung resolution. It is not for me to-day to argue, still less to criticise. We have to encourage to action those who are fully persuaded in their own minds: to whom the three orders of ministry in the Church are Scriptural primitive essentials. For us the form of government, the authority, ministrations, liturgy, teaching, sacraments, the canon of Scripture; again, the spiritual priesthood of the laity, our bulwark against Papacy, our anchor amid sects, are knit all together and indissolubly attached to this unbroken historic thread.

Anciently, the vital value of this thread to the life of the Church was understood so well that the model persecutor Decius, whose characteristic was "his knowledge and foresight on every subject," when he entered on his enterprise of suppressing the Church, published simply an edict against the Bishops. For modern England, the whole thought of the practical life of the Church is so tied up to our triple ministry, that, whenever this Church of ours has lacked Episcopacy, in our colonies or on our Mission field, the work has languished. Wherever it is established the work both spreads and deepens. This result may be ascribed (by those who will) to the mere fact that our organizations have received such an impress of Episcopacy that without it they are imperfect and so become unfruitful. There are other ways of accounting for it also, which (as I said) we need not discuss; but the fact is patent and its leading evident.

And now, on this Commemoration Day, may I tell the tale of what we commemorate? It will not take long; but seeing that some of our largest popular histories are innocent of the least mention of it, I would fain tell it over like some household memory at this gathering of the families.

Our great American colonies and states had, partly from their antecedents, partly by policies here, been kept until a century ago dependent for their Church government, as for other things, on England. Three thousand miles of ocean was a wide space between Christian flocks and their Bishops. Ordinations were only in England — at heavy cost — not without many perils. Confirmations were none. Ruling and direction such as we may imagine. Little by little the Church was drooping into decay. Indeed it was in captivity — in fragments. " Our scattered, wandering, and sinking Church" are the pathetic words in which they described their own condition. Some of the congregations had grown indifferent. Some of the political leaders were bitterly hostile. Fatal reminiscences made many religious people implacable.

Appendices

Religious organization was employed not to promote religion, but to assail the Church. Let me illustrate from a contemporary letter the efforts, whose utter failure may comfort some failing spirit disposed to quail at what it fancies to be "signs of the times." It refers to as much as thirty years before the date we speak of. "Even then it was evident from the continued publications in the newspapers, and from the unity of all the jarring interests of Independents, and Presbyterians, from Massachusetts to Georgia, under grand committees and synods, that some mischievous action was meditated against the Church." Many had labored, many had suffered for the ever baffled hope of completing the truncated constitution of their Church. When at last the great severance came there were two voices from her Churchmen. One was of despair. "Now every hope is over, we can never inherit the succession of the fatherland. We must elect to ourselves men whom we can make titular nominal Bishops for good order's sake. The oil of Aaron must be done without — it is denied us for ever." The other cry invoked hope even against hope. They appealed yet again to the Bishops of England. "If you could not give us your succession before, when we were fellow-subjects, because British legislation had given you no enabling power on our behalf, then at least bestow it on us now as fellow-Christians, yes, fellow-Churchmen, whom no war can sever from unity in Christ, whom no statutes now afflict with disability." There was no answer. The moment is thus described by a contemporary with a not intemperate indignation. "I am at a loss to understand why considerations of a purely political kind should have had such enervating influence on the English Bishops as to render them passive spectators of the destitution of their American children." It seemed to some as if, half living flesh, half marble, like the stricken priests in the Arabian tale we filled our chairs, feeling willing, but motionless. We know now how some hearts had long been beating high to help.[1] How Tenison, Gibson, Butler, Sherlock, Secker, Terrick, Lowth, had given means and had given toil, had reasoned with men and prayed to God, how a Berkeley had sacrificed all that he had for the hope of obtaining pastors for them.

There are those who think it the point of honor with sons to "sling at their fathers and not miss." I pray rather that we may overcome some difficulties of our own, before which we stand halting, as fairly as they mastered theirs. Think of Statutes which tacitly precluded the imparting of our Church constitution to the children of our Church; immense legal ingenuity closing every avenue to independence; a throne foreign to our Church, only slowly growing amicable to her; memories which made the whole nation revolt from the thought of the Crown's exercising a dispensing power; cabinets which accounted the offices of the Church to be the cheapest bribes they could offer to the world, and thought it a feat of "wisdom" to have silenced Convocation. When we are so sure that we should not have been as our fathers, a few candid minutes spent in considering what has become of the leaden weights which oppressed them and who removed them, might leave us doubtful in another sense whether we shall hereafter deserve such thanks as we owe to them.

[1] See the *Bishop of St. Andrews' Address* (Blackwood, 1884), p. 12. Archbishop Tenison died A. D. 1715, Bishop Lowth, 1787.

Appendices

When at last revolution might seem to have burst the bonds, there appeared a fresh illegality in duty and charity; to adapt the letter to the spirit of the service-book was impossible; the oath to the English Sovereign was essential to the consecration of a Bishop by Bishops. An episcopal Church seemed compelled to compel an episcopal Church to be Presbyterian. Say rather a crisis seemed at hand when prelates would once more have to choose between the law of man and the Gospel of Christ. I for one am certain how such men would have chosen had it come to this. But once more in the Church's history God committed deliverance not to the strong but to the smallest and feeblest of all.

The third person of the drama, the Church once "of Scotland," was in the dust. Her Officers and her Offices lay under terrible disabilities. Legislation had recently attempted to annihilate even what a writer of the times properly called "her shattered remains.[1]" She worshipped under penal statutes, the more insulting because no one would now have executed them. Still she could not emerge from back streets and upper floors. And the poor remnant of her Bishops, four in number, lived, driven into one diocese, in poverty and in piety.

Her very existence was a breach of law, like that of a Church of the first days under a humane emperor. Her holiest acts were offences, the more sacred the more criminal. She was asked to undertake what the Church of England was not strong enough to effect. And thus she answered in the person of one of her poor prelates: "Considering

[1] Bishop Jolly, *Letter to Bishop Kemp; Documents issued by the Historical Club of the American Church*, No. 19.

the great *depositum* committed to us, I do not see how we can account to our great Lord and Master if we neglect such an opportunity of promoting His truth and enlarging the borders of His Church." So then, while the new States eyed Episcopacy with a suspicious hate that had its roots in the past, and believed it to be irreconcilable with the interests of a Republic, little knowing what strength it had lent to every form of government in its turn; while the idea of it seemed, alas! so lost in State-craft that even the Church of America itself partly doubted for a while whether its orders were certainly valid, as having been conferred without the consent of a State; while a proposal was being ventilated for a nominal Episcopacy created by lay and clerical votes; while our Lord Chancellor was instructing the House of Lords that the Episcopal clergy for other countries should be ordained by English and Irish prelates only — while such were the "counsels of princes," the feeble remnant in Scotland was quietly facing the crisis of the Church of the future. Humbly and peacefully, with knowledge of what they were doing, they laid their hands on the chosen man in an upper chamber, and imparted to the New World the gift of "a free, valid and purely ecclesiastical Episcopacy." These were their own words, "free, valid, and purely ecclesiastical." It is no wonder that those ringing words sound again and again in the letters of that time, and that they were incorporated in the "beloved concordat" which ruled the relations of Scotland and America.

The man, too, was worthy for whom they should do this. He has been characterized as "a simple, grand, conciliatory, uncompromising man."[1] His

[1] Chief Justice Shea.

noble portrait answers to the double antithesis. The expression is gentle of features which have no slight stamp of the heroic. He had the courage of humility. He was honest, patient, ready to put himself out of sight if the cause could be better served by his being forgotten. The gifts which rouse personal enthusiasm seldom accompany so solid a nature. Yet we read (strangely as it sounds) that his preaching "to an amazing throng of people on the Atonement was so striking that it was almost impossible to restrain the audience from loud shouts of approbation." Conciliation without compromise, the yielding unyielding presence of an elastic spring, never withdrawn, never rigid, is the image of his action. He had known what it was to suffer for his opinions and his courage. He had been seized by armed men, dragged some seventy miles, paraded through the streets, lain six weeks in gaol, his home pillaged, his children beaten, himself left destitute. No bitterness broke from him. Injustice strengthened his purpose and nourished his sweetness. "I am determined," he writes, on his return, "to stay here as long as I am permitted to discharge the duties of my Mission, whatever personal inconvenience it may subject me to. It is God's property to bring order out of confusion, good out of evil, and may His will be done."

"Nulla ecclesia sine episcopo" was the motto which he early placed under his shield, looking on the vastness of his country,[1] divining its grandeur,

---

[1] "The union of the Church of England and the Episcopal Church of America . . . must be of great advantage to the Church in America, and may also be so at some future period to the Church of England." — *Bishop Seabury's Letter to the Society for the Propagation of the Gospel*, Feb. 27, 1784.

inspired with the sense of his Church's future, and certain that it was all in all for her that her *primitiæ* should be *primitivæ;* her first fruits like those of the first days.

The revenges of God are orderly and beautiful. They light on men and places with an exactitude we cannot mistake. Seabury's first sermon as Bishop in his own land was preached in the pulpit of Bishop Berkeley,[1] our own Confessor for the American Church. The State whose gaol inflicted his humiliation was Connecticut; he reëntered its chief city as its chief pastor and Father in God. But in deeper things than mere outward arresting signs we realize the presence and unity of God's purpose. Surely it was a great honor, a broad seal of His own, which was put on the Church of America for ever in these events by God, that she should have been turned back from the grand portals which were close to her and bidden to enter by so strait a gate on the wondrous inheritance of which but a small part even now is hers. What had hindered that the purposes of her first founders should be fulfilled? How was it she was not born to great endowments? Why not at least to her natural position of establishment with its great opportunities and great obligations? Why did not the full stream of the English Church flow in on her, and advance smooth and broad, evenly with the population and the institutions? It can surely have been only because the first mark of sonship in spiritual life is chastisement — because the mother of power is humility — because the yoke is borne in youth by all those whose manhood is free indeed. Is it possible that a really great Church should be able

[1] At Newport.

to enter into the secret of her apostleship without the searching, fiery disciplines which have seared with pain the whole frame of the Church, not only in her first days, but wherever she has made a new beginning, or reasserted herself in her purity? It is not for her to move on in the dauntless, heedless pride of nations born in a day. She must not be deceived into receiving kingdoms and the glory of them as a free gift. She must conquer them by some conformity to the Passion of her Lord. No surer token has any Church ever received that He is the same yesterday, to-day, and for ever, than the Church of America — destined within a century to found her sixty-seven sees — received in being, against all anticipations or probabilities, constrained to begin from the very beginning, stripped of essentials, and thankful to receive them from the least and most "suffering Church"[1] of the whole earth.

Church of America! Because the Lord loved thee, He humbled thee, and suffered thee to hunger, that He might prove thee. Lovingly, and according to thy strength, He laid His Cross upon thee. *In hoc signo vinces.*

And now there are three simple lessons which, it seems to me, the holy joyfulness of the chain of greetings from Woodbury to Aberdeen, and the sober splendors of this our solemn anniversary, lay upon the heart and memory of our Churches until the next centenary shall come round with perhaps wholly new lessons.

I. The first is patience: Church patience; patience with God: the patience of a waiting spouse, growing more intensely His by reason of anxiety; less and

[1] Dr. Berkeley, Beardsley's *Life of Seabury* (London, Hodges, p. 105).

less able to think of anything but His coming — and utterly sure of Him. To fast, to pray, to implore His presence, to watch for sound or token. But never, never to do that which it is His prerogative to do at His own time. Never to take what it is His to give.

There is something thrilling in the last quarter of the year 1784. Years of prayer and waiting had gone by; tears and suffering had been spent; and still there was no sign. And one great leader of religious feeling lost patience. He had set stagnant waters flowing in channels new and old. He had rekindled slumbering sparks of devotion. He had organized languor and torpor into life. For America how he had prayed and labored. Church order had been his first yearning, America his first field. How he had trusted that the English Church would give her Bishops, complete her structure and her powers. At last he would wait no longer. His own end could not be very distant. Was he to die and leave her still without a deacon, priest, or bishop of her own, without Consecrations, without the binding seal and stirring grace of Confirmation? No sooner had he answered that question in his own way by his own act than the clouds removed. What he did is well known. And he did it in that memorable year 1784, on the 2d of September. On the 14th of November Seabury was consecrated.

After an interval of less than eleven weeks America possessed the "free, valid, and purely ecclesiastical supremacy" for which John Wesley prayed but for which he would not wait.

II. It is a lesson in being content with the essence, and despising the most desirable accompaniments, whenever true solutions of Church problems present themselves. It teaches us the true value to the Church of the "present difficulty," whatever it be. The supreme importance of solving it rightly and of waiting till some right solution comes, but also of accepting whatever legitimate solution becomes possible in God's providence, even though the accompaniments of it fall far short of what we hoped.

The most fruitful of thinkers tells us that his method was to set before himself with the utmost clearness the conditions of his problem — to hold them, as it were, in solution in his mind, and keep them constantly present to himself, and that then gradually light dawned. The wisdom of Churchmen in dealing with many Church problems is the same — to keep the conditions steadily before them until light dawns. There were at that time two leading conditions. They had to continue the Church on the primitive model; they had to win men into Christ. There was the continuous building, construction, extension — "edification" St. Paul calls it — of the Church on the Apostolic plan only; no obliteration permissible. There was the conciliation of men through studying the spirit of the age, understanding it, reckoning with it.

We may not depart from the ancient ground plan, the vision shown in the Mount, or we shall find ourselves building a Babylon, not a Sion. We may not give up the "persuading of men," "the commending ourselves to all men," or we shall find ourselves building void sanctuaries and desolate cloisters. The American fathers looked to something beyond, the establishing themselves in popular estimation at a time when English Churchmanship was on all sides thought incompatible with fresh forms of government. They would not please men at the cost of abandoning the catholic exemplar. They would not please themselves. They had longed to receive the institution they desired invested with the *prestige*, the deep grandeur, the solemnities of their mother Church. But, dear as those were to them (how dear let the Christian ballads of their Church Poet witness); dear as they were, it was not those which they desired, but the inner soul and core of the primæval rule. And this dwelt as well with poverty and the world's spite in an upper room as in the glorious gloom of a Westminster, or by the solidity of deep-founded thrones. It was poverty, it was confessorship, it was almost outlawry, which offered them the answer of God, and they took it with tears of joy. They were fain to seek God's kingdom in Christ's way, and presently all else was added to them.

III. The third lesson is that the dawn we spoke of came, and that always it must come, through the inherent power of high principles — a firm faith in the possibility of distinguishing better from worse, a fast hold of what has been committed to us, however scorned or attacked. It is not noisy proclamation which works. The leaven and the seed are the types of the kingdom. An intense force resides in any single living truth, held, spoken, lived in simplicity. In the quiet, unenthusiastic style of the time Archbishop Secker had years before described the need of more outspoken doctrine and fuller expression of Church thought. Some might smile at the extreme moderation of his tone; but it may be remembered that it was an age in which "enthusiasm" was the equivalent term for fanaticism: when young clergy

Appendices

were counselled not to dwell too much on the work of the Holy Spirit; and the town was placarded with terror of Rome because Bishop Porteus recommended that Good Friday should be observed. In 1760 then Secker writes — "It hath been a pretty general defect among us that we have not insisted sufficiently in our discourses on the peculiar doctrines of Christianity, nor enforced sufficiently our practical exhortations with peculiarly Christian motives. We [should] dwell oftener on the fallen condition of men, on the efficacy of faith, and the necessity of sanctifying grace."[1] Again, "No one hath more at heart the establishment of Bishops in America. Few persons, if any, have taken more pains to convince those on whom it depends of the need and usefulness of it. But the time for it is not yet come. God grant it may soon. . . . Dispose the laity to desire it." Truly no leaven was ever at work more noiselessly. But it did work. And because it was true seed, it mattered not that it was the least of seeds. Who would have believed that the faithful action of the Scottish Bishops on so small a scale would have been followed in eighteen months by the Act of Parliament[2] which gave in fullest measure all that had ever been desired, all that for high reasons of State the great ministers of Great Britain had again and again refused. So, when Cyprian in the unlawful assembly of his Bishops at Carthage quietly sketched the course they would adopt and then wait for the judgment of the "Lord Jesus Christ" upon it, "Who singly and

[1] Archbishop Secker, *Letter to Dr. Smith*, October 12, 1760, *Historical Documents* (7).

[2] "We should never have obtained the succession from England, had he (Bishop Seabury) or some other not have obtained it first from Scotland." — Mr. Parker of Boston, *ap*. Beardsley, p. 211.

alone" (said he) "hath the power to advance us in the governance of His Church, and pass judgment upon our action,"[1]—when he so said, Episcopacy was ready to take its place (nay, may it not be said to have taken its place already?) among the institutions of the Roman Empire. It had only now to be recognized. Every confiscation, every martyrdom, only secured it a higher, firmer footing.

But, oh, brethren, it is not for Episcopacy's sake that we keep this festival together. That is, indeed, the heading of the one page we have turned to-day. But the glory of Catholic religion is, while giving full meaning and efficacy to every organic detail, still never to confuse the organs with the body or with the life. The organs are not the Church. The Church is not for the organs; but the organs are for the Church and the Gospel, for the Christ of the Gospel and of the Church. It is just because He is all in all to us; because He is not only above everything to us, but is in everything and everything in Him, that we are able to insist on the presence of His Divine power in all His institutions and all their operation.

One versed in human nature, one who can speak of his experience of men as ranging from the Canton to the Hudson's river, said the other day that what all his experience led him most to urge was "the belief in an attainable high standard of morality for all men." "Disbelief," he said,[2] "in that attainable high standard of morality was at the root of international hatreds and hostilities," "making men suspicious of their fellows." Where there is no faith in

[1] Sentt. Epp. Syn. Carth. sub Cyp. vii. "Cyprianus dixit," etc.
[2] Sir F. Goldsmid, Carlisle Church Congress, 1884.

man there can be no faith in God. Where there is
no love of God there is no love of souls. To us that
faith in the attainable high morality of all men is
simply faith in Christ. We believe that all men can
have Him and all in Him. The faith of Christ is no
longer a progressive school of thought. The faith
is already face to face with mankind in all lands.
Within the Church, those evangelical teachings of
which great Churchmen a hundred years ago spoke
as nearly ignored have had free course. Doctrines
yet closer to our Lord's own Person, the fullness with
which His Incarnation charges all thoughts, all
things, the abundance of His Atonement, His Resurrection Life are (we have reason to know) closer to
the hearts of men. His Presence grows more of a
reality to many lives. History, criticism, science,
have not been at work in vain. They have introduced higher intelligence, deeper reality into our
grasp of doctrine. His Person and His present Life
have a known felt power. Without the doctrine
faith is not Christian faith, morals are but heathen
morals. We know the worth and work not only of
the old ethics, but of the old worships. But when
their all was spent Christ came. It was the fullness
of time. Time was ripe for Him, the world was
ready, and we too have reached a crisis of history
when the full, brimming Church is able to deal with
every race, to pour the faith of Christ over the whole
earth. It is the history of England and of America
which reveals the prospect. Not their ecclesiastical
history alone (although Seabury's successors are a
hundred and thirty-nine, and the seven foreign bishoprics which depended on England have become
seventy-five since our Queen began to reign), but the

far wider aspects and preparations of their past. From what basis was England's place in the world of empire won? Once she called nothing her own but her situation only. Geographical position — she possessed nothing else. She literally fulfilled the boast of the ancient mathematician, "Give me a place to stand on and I will move the earth." She had a rock-pedestal in the world of waters and no more. But the history of America opens out in an age when continental areas, lately intractable for vastness, are by mere acceleration of movement endowed with all the facilities of smallness. The Atlantic and Pacific shores are not so far apart as once our own channels were. And to this add all things without limit — territory unlimited — nations born in an hour to people it — difficulties overwhelming, yet practically no limit to the resources which believing populations can devote to the Master's service.

Two dangers to religion might have been feared within. You might have been tempted to a selfish despair, " no hope of evangelizing such multitudes — therefore confine all work to home — be content to be a pure primitive sect," — or that other temptation of the multitude, "regard the corporate life only — the individualizing of souls is not your vocation." The divine instinct which moves you to covet those two titles, "The most missionary Church," "The Church of the poorest," saves and will save you from both temptations.

The " high attainable standard," then, it is ours to advance. We are to believe that Christ is attainable for all souls, — or rather that all souls are attainable by Christ. A crisis is ours to direct such as time has never known before, and its very earthliest vehicle and means is a language and a view of politics which are fast girdling the globe. Gazing on the last hundred years, with their failures and their sins, yet seeing how His cause has kept advancing, not at mere even pace, but with accelerating velocity, and that at once in all directions the mind fails in attempting to conceive what one more Christian century will have worked. When our times are left as far behind as Seabury's are now, may we be found to have secured a harvest in proportion to his! Yet it ought to be so, for if he is the man whom God, the God of the spirits of all flesh, set up over His congregation, that the congregation of the Lord might not be as sheep having no shepherd, ours, on the other hand, is that Catholic Church which St. John saw ride multitudinous across the sky, conquering and to conquer. This is that Church which long since unhorsed the spectres of superstition that had ridden side by side with them out of heathenism, and has humbly striven to be true to Him Whose name is the Word of God. Oh, for soldiers to muster thick and fast behind such Leader! We live at a moment when zeal and self-denial could do anything if they would come to the fore; when fiery men, hard men, who could suffer hardness, who would equip themselves to a true measure of fitness, who would delight in wisdom and innocence, who would be content with food and raiment, could work miracles.

We dare not cease to utter the call, though our own call is so different a one. We abide here not for ease; but they would pass like night from land to land. They would have strange power of speech. Has it not been proved? They would teach their tale to ears willing and unwilling. They would leave the "high attainable standard" attained behind them as they passed. For Christ Himself would be given and be received. In all humility we say it. It cannot be vain on Seabury's Day to say it.

Documents

RELATING TO THE EPISCOPAL SUCCESSION

AND THE

CONSECRATION

OF

SAMUEL SEABURY.

The Concordat

IN THE NAME OF THE HOLY AND UNDIVIDED TRINITY, FATHER, SON, AND HOLY GHOST, ONE GOD BLESSED FOR EVER; AMEN:—

The wise and gracious Providence of this mercifull God, having put it into the hearts of the Christians of the Episcopal persuasion in Connecticut in North America, to desire that the Blessings of a free, valid and purely Ecclesiastical Episcopacy, might be communicated to them, and a Church regularly formed in that part of the western world upon the most antient, and primitive Model: And application having been made for this purpose, by the Reverend Dr. Samuel Seabury, Presbyter in Connecticut, to the Right Reverend the Bishops of the Church in Scotland: The said Bishops having taken this proposal into their serious Consideration, most heartily concurred to promote and encourage the same, as far as lay in their power; and accordingly began the pious and good work recommended to them, by complying with the request of the Clergy in Connecticut, and advancing the said Dr. Samuel Seabury to the high Order of the Episcopate; At the same time earnestly praying that this Work of the Lord thus happily begun might prosper in his hands, till it should please the great and glorious Head of the Church, to increase the number of Bishops in America, and send forth more such Labourers into that part of his Harvest. — Animated with this pious hope, and earnestly desirous to establish a Bond of peace, and holy Communion, between the two Churches, the Bishops of the Church in Scotland, whose names are underwritten, having had full and free Conference with Bishop Seabury, after his Consecration and Advancement as aforesaid, agreed with him on the following Articles, which are to serve as a Concordate, or Bond of Union, between the Catholic remainder of the antient Church of Scotland, and the now rising Church in the State of Connecticut.

Art. I. They agree in thankfully receiving, and humbly and heartily embracing the whole Doctrine of the Gospel, as revealed and set forth in the holy Scriptures: and it is their earnest and united Desire to maintain the Analogy of the common Faith, once delivered to the Saints, and happily preserved in the Church of Christ, thro his divine power and protection, who promised that the Gates of Hell should never prevail against it.

Art. II. They agree in believing this Church to be the mystical Body of Christ, of which he alone is the Head, and supreme Governour, and that under him, the chief Ministers, or Managers of the Affairs of this spiritual Society, are those called Bishops, whose Exercise of their sacred Office being independent on all Lay powers, it follows of consequence, that their spiritual Authority and Jurisdiction cannot be affected by any Lay-Deprivation.

Art. III. They agree in declaring that the Episcopal Church in Connecticut is to be in full Communion with the Episcopal Church in Scotland, it being their sincere Resolution to put matters on such a footing, as that the Members of both Churches may with freedom and safety communicate with either, when their Occasions call them from the one Country to the other: Only taking Care when in Scotland not to hold Communion in sacred Offices with those persons, who under pretence of Ordination by an English, or Irish Bishop, do, or shall take, upon them, to officiate as Clergymen in any part of the National Church of Scotland, and whom the Scottish Bishops cannot help looking upon, as schismatical Intruders, designed only to answer worldly purposes, and uncommissioned Disturbers of the poor Remains of that once flourishing Church, which both their predecessors and they, have, under many Difficulties, laboured to preserve pure and uncorrupted to future Ages.

Art. IV. With a view to the salutary purpose mentioned in the preceding Article, they agree in desiring that there may be as near a Conformity in Worship, and Discipline established between the two Churches as is consistent with the different Circumstances and Customs of Nations: And in order to avoid any bad effects that might otherwise arise from political Differences, they hereby express their earnest Wish and firm Intention to observe such prudent Generality in their public Prayers, with respect to these points, as shall appear most agreeable to Apostolic Rules, and the practice of the primitive Church.

Art. V. As the Celebration of the holy Eucharist, or the Administration of the Sacrament of the Body and Blood of Christ, is the principal Bond of Union among Christians, as well as the most Solemn Act of Worship in the Christian Church, the Bishops aforesaid agree in desiring that there may be as little Variance here as possible. And tho' the Scottish Bishops are very far from prescribing to their Brethren in this matter, they cannot help ardently wishing that Bishop Seabury would endeavour all he can consistently with peace and prudence, to make the Celebration of this venerable Mystery conformable to the most primitive Doctrine and practice in that respect: Which is the pattern the Church of Scotland has copied after in her Communion Office, and which it has been the Wish of some of the most eminent Divines of the Church of England that she also had more closely followed, than she seems to have done since she gave up her first reformed Liturgy used in the Reign of King Edward VI.; between which, and the form used in the Church of Scotland, there is no Difference in any point, which the primitive Church reckoned essential to the right Ministration of the holy Eucharist. — In this capital Article therefore of the Eucharistic Service, in which the Scottish Bishops so earnestly wish for as much Unity as possible, Bishop Seabury also agrees to take a serious View of the Communion Office recommended by them, and if found agreeable to the genuine Standards of Antiquity, to give his Sanction to it, and by gentle Methods of Argument and Persuasion, to endeavour, as they have done, to introduce it by degrees into practice without the Compulsion of Authority on the one side, or the predjudice of former Custom on the other.

Art. VI. It is also hereby agreed and resolved upon for the better answering the purposes of this Concordate, that a brotherly fellowship be henceforth maintained between the Episcopal Churches in

Scotland and Connecticut, and such a mutual Intercourse of Ecclesiastical Correspondence carried on, when Opportunity offers, or necessity requires as may tend to the Support, and Edification of both Churches.

Art. VII. The Bishops aforesaid do hereby jointly declare, in the most solemn manner, that in the whole of this Transaction, they have nothing else in view, but the Glory of God, and the good of his Church; And being thus pure and upright in their Intentions, they cannot but hope, that all whom it may concern, will put the most fair and candid construction on their Conduct, and take no Offence at their feeble, but sincere Endeavours to promote what they believe to be the Cause of Truth, and of the common Salvation.

In Testimony of their Love to which, and in mutual good Faith and Confidence, they have for themselves, and their Successors in Office cheerfully put their Names and Seals to these presents at Aberdeen this fifteenth day of November, in the year of our Lord, one thousand, seven hundred, and eighty-four.

   ROBERT KILGOUR, Bishop & Primus. [SEAL.]
   ARTHUR PETRIE, Bishop. [SEAL.]
   JOHN SKINNER, JR., Bishop. [SEAL.]
   SAMUEL SEABURY, Bishop. [SEAL.]

RELATING TO THE SCOTS EPISCOPACY AS
CONNECTED WITH THE ENGLISH EPISCOPACY,
AND WITH THE CONSECRATION OF
BISHOP SEABURY.

Extract from the Register of Archbishop Juxon, in the Library of his Grace the Archbishop of Canterbury, at Lambeth Palace. — Fol. 237.

IT appears that James Sharp was consecrated Archbishop of St. Andrew's — Andrew Fairfoull, Archbishop of Glasgow — Robert Leighton, Bishop of Doublenen (Dunblane) — and James Hamilton, Bishop of Galloway — on the 15th day of December, 1661, in St. Peter's Church, Westminster, by Gilbert, Bishop of London, Commissary to the Archbishop of Canterbury; — and that the Right Rev. George, Bishop of Worcester, John, Bishop of Carlisle, and Hugh, Bishop of Landaff, were present and assisting.

Extracted this 3d day of June, 1789, *by me,*
WILLIAM DICKES, Secretary.

London, June 3d, 1789.

THAT the above is a true copy of an extract procured by order of Archbishop Moore, to be sent to Bishop Seabury, in Connecticut, is attested by us, Bishops of the Scottish Church, now in this place, on business of importance to the said Church.

JOHN SKINNER, Bishop.
WILLIAM ABERNETHY DRUMMOND, Bishop.
JOHN STRÆCHAN, Bishop.

The following is taken from the original and officially attested list, given to Bishop Seabury himself, of the Consecration and succession of Bishops so far as his own Consecration is concerned: and has been by me personally compared with that original, now in the possession of the Reverend William Jones Seabury, D. D., of New York.

      [Signed] GEORGE SHEA.
September 12, 1892.

BISHOP HICKE'S SUCCESSION DEDUCED:

1693. Feb. 23. Dr George Hickes was consecrated Suffragan of Thetford, in the Bishop of Peterborough's Chapel in the Parish of Enfield, by Dr William Loyd, B'p of Norwich, Dr Francis Turner, B'p of Ely, and Dr Thomas White B'p of Peterborough.[1]

1675. July 4. Dr William Loyd was consecrated B'p of Landaff, in Lambeth Chapel by Dr Gilbert Sheldon A. Bp of Canterbury, Dr Richard Stearn A. B'p of York & Dr Peter Gunning B'p of Ely. He was translated to Peterborough May 17. 1679, & thence to Norwich July 4, 1685.

1683. Aug. 27. Dr Francis Turner was consecrated B'p of Rochester in Lambeth Chapel, by Dr William Sancroft A. B'p of Canterbury, Dr Henry Compton B'p of London, Dr Nathanael Crew B'p of Durham, Dr Seth Ward B'p of Sarum, &

---

[1] Dr Loyd, Dr Turner and Dr White were three of the English Bishops who were deprived at the Revolution, by the civic power, for not swearing allegiance to William the Third. They were also three of the seven Bishops who had been sent to the Tower, by James the Second, for refusing to order an illegal proclamation to be read in their dioceses.

D' William Loyd B'p of Peterborough. He was translated to Ely, Aug. 23. 1684.

1685. July 25. D' Thomas White was consecrated B'p of Peterborough in Lambeth Chapel by A. B'p Sancroft, B'p Compton of London, B'p Turner of Ely, D' William Loyd, B'p of S' Asaph, D' John Lake B'p of Chichester, D' Thomas Sprat B'p of Dunkeld in Scotland.

B'P LOYD OF NORWICH'S CONSECRATORS:

1660. Oct. 28. D' Sheldon was consecrated B'p of London in K. Henry the 7ths Chapel at Westminster, by B'pps & D⁰ˢ Brian Duppa of Winchester, Accepted Trewen of York, Matthew Wren of Ely, John Warner of Rochester, & Henry King of Chichester, by Commission from A. B'p Juxon of Canterbury, whom he succeeded & was confirmed in that See in Lambeth Chapel Aug. 31. 1663.

1660. Dec. 2. In the same Chapel, & by a like Commission was consecrated D' Richard Stearn to the See of Carlisle, by B'p Sheldon of London, B'p Duppa of Winchester, D' Humphrey Henchman B'p of Salisbury, and D' Robert Sanderson B'p of Lincoln. He was translated to York, June 10. 1664.

1669. Mar. 6. D' Peter Gunning was consecrated B'p of Chichester by A. Bps Sheldon & Stearn, B'p Henchman of London, D' George Morley of Winchester, Benjamin Lamy of Ely, Seth Ward of Sarum, John Dolbin of Rochester & Anthony Sparrow of Exeter B'pps. He was translated to Ely, Mar. 4. 1675.

ARCH. B'P SHELDON'S CONSECRATORS.

1638. May 4. Dr Brian Duppa was promoted to the See of Chichester, but the Consecrators Names, nor Time, nor Place of his Consecration have not been found. In 1641 he was translated to Salisbury, & Octr 4. 1660 to Winchester.

1641. Decr 19. Dr Henry King was consecrated B'p of Chichester, by whom, or where has not been found.

1644. April . Dr Accepted Trewen was consecrated Bp of Litchfield & Coventry in Magdalene College Chapel, by Dr John Williams A. B'p of York, Drs Walter Curl of Winchester, Robert Skinner of Oxford, Brian Duppa of Salisbury, & John Towers of Peterborough Bishops. He was confirmed A. Bp of York Oct'r 4. 1660.

1634. March 8. Dr Matthew Wren was consecrated Bp of Hereford in Lambeth Chapel by A. B'p Laud, Dr Richard Neil A. B'p of York, Dr Walter Curl of Winchester, Dr Francis White of Ely, Dr Joseph Hall of Exeter & Dr William Murray of Landaff B'ps. He was translated to Norwich Dec'r 1635, thence to Ely Apr. 24. 1638.

1637. Jan. 14. Dr John Warner was consecrated Bp of Rochester in Lambeth Chapel by A. Bp Laud, Dr William Juxon Bp of London, Dr Walter Curl Bp of Winchester, Dr John Bancroft Bp of Oxford, and William Roberts B'p of Bangor.

B'P STEARN'S CONSECRATORS,

Of A. Bp Sheldon & Bp Duppa already:

1660. Octr 28. Dr Henchman was consecrated Bp of Salisbury, & Dr Sanderson Bp of Lincoln, at the same Time & Place, & by the same Persons with Bp Sheldon. Dr Henchman was translated to London Septr 15. 1663.

BP GUNNING'S CONSECRATORS,

Of Bps Sheldon, Stearn, & Henchman already:

1660. Oct^t 28. Dr George Morley was consecrated Bp of Worcester with Bp Sheldon &c as above. He was translated to Winchester May 4. 1662.

1660. Dec. 2. Dr Benjamin Lany was consecrated Bp of Peterborough with Bp Stearn as above. He was translated to Lincoln Apr. 2. 1663. and from thence to Ely, June 12. 1667.

1666. July 1. Dr John Dolben was consecrated in Lambeth Chapel by A. Bps Sheldon & Stearn, Bpps Henchman of London, Morley of Winchester, Lany of Lincoln, & John Halket Bp of Litchfield & Coventry.

1667. Novr 3. Dr Anthony Sparrow was consecrated at Lambeth by A. Bp Sheldon, Bpps Morley of Winchester, & Lany of Ely, Dr William Nicolson Bp of Glocester, Dr Seth Ward Bp of Salisbury, Dr Robert Morgan Bp of Bangor, & Dr William Fuller Bp of Lincoln.

ARTHUR PETRIE, Clerk.[1]

---

[1] One of the consecrators of Samuel Seabury, Nov. 14, 1785.

The Scots Bishops

N. B. *Bishop Hicke's Consecration is deduced as goes before, on account of his being concerned in the Consecration of the Scottish Bishops according to the following List:*

LIST OF CONSECRATIONS IN SCOTLAND, WITH THE TRUE DATES, & CONSECRATORS NAMES, AS FAR AS THE PRESENT BISHOPS ARE CONCERNED.

1705. Jan. 25. Mr John Sage, formerly one of the Ministers of Glasgow, and Mr John Fullarton, formerly Minister of Paisley, were consecrated at Edinburgh, by John Paterson. A. Bp of Glasgow, Alexander Rose Bp of Edinburgh, & Robert Douglas Bp of Dunblane.[1]

1709. April 28. Mr John Falconar, Minister at Cairnbee, & Mr Henry Chrystie Minister at Kinross, were consecrated at Dundee, by Bp Rose of Edin^r, Bp Douglas of Dunblane, and Bp Sage.

1711. Aug. 25. The Honourable Archibald Campbel was consecrated at Dundee by Bp Rose of Edin^r Bishop Douglas of Dunblane, & Bp Falconar.

1712. Febr. 24. Mr James Gadderar formerly Minister at Kilmaurs was consecrated at London, by Bp Hickes, Bp Falconar, & Bp Campbel.

1718. Oct. 22. Mr Arthur Millar formerly Minister at Inveresk, and Mr William Irvine, formerly Minister at Kirkmichael in Carriet, were consecrated at Edin^r by Bp Rose of Ed^r, Bpps Fullarton & Falconar.

---

[1] Archbishop Paterson, Bishop Rose and Bishop Douglas, were deprived at the Revolution, by the civil power, for, also, not swearing allegiance to William the Third.

AFTER THE BISHOP OF EDINʀ's DEATH:

1722. Oct. 17. Mʳ Andrew Cant, formerly one of the Ministers of Edʳ & Mʳ David Freebairn formerly Minister at Dunning, were consecrated at Edinʳ by Bp Fullarton, Bp Millar, & Bp Irvine.

1727. June 4. Dʳ Thomas Rattray of Craighall was consecrated at Edinʳ by Bp Gadderar, Bp Millar, & Bp Cant.

1727. June 18. Mʳ William Dunbar Minister at Cruden, & Mʳ Robert Keith Presbyter in Edinʳ were consecrated at Edinburgh, by Bp Gadderar, Bp Millar, & Bp Rattray.

1735. June 24. Mʳ Robert White Presbyter at Cupar, was consecrated at Carsebank near Forfar, by Bp Rattray, Bp Dunbar, and Bp Keith.

1741. Sept. 10. Mʳ William Falconar Presbyter at Forress was consecrated at Alloa in Clacmannan Shire, by Bp Rattray, Bp Keith & Bp White.

1742. Oct. 4. Mʳ James Rait Presbyter at Dundee, was consecrated at Edinburgh, by Bp Rattray, Bp Keith, & Bp White.

1743. Aug. 19. Mʳ John Alexander Presbyter at Alloa in Clacmannanshire, was consecrated at Edinburgh, by Bp Keith, Bp White, Bp Falconar & Bp Raitt.

1747. July 17. Mʳ Andrew Gerard Presbyter in Aberdeen, was consecrated at Cupar in Fife, by Bp White, Bp Falconar, Bp Rait & Bp Alexander.

1759. Nov'r. 1. Mʳ Henry Edgar was consecrated at the same Place, & by the same Bishops as Coadjutor to Bp White then Primus.

The Scots Bishops 97

1762. June 24. M' Robert Forbes was consecrated at Forfar by Bpps Falconar. Primus, Alexander, & Gerard.

1768. Sept. 21. M' Robert Kilgour Presbyter at Peterhead was consecrated Bishop of Aberdeen at Cupar in Fife, by Bp Falconar Primus, Bp Rait, and Bp Alexander.

1774. Aug. 24. M' Charles Rose Presbyter at Down was consecrated Bishop of Dunblane, at Forfar by Bp Falconar Primus, Bp Rait Bp Forbes.

1776. June 27. M' Arthur Petrie, Presbyter at Meiklefolla was consecrated Bishop Co-adjutor, at Dundee, by Bp Falconar Primus, Bp Rait, Bp Kilgour, & Bp Rose. And appointed Bishop of Ross & Caithness July 8. 1777.

1778. Aug. 13. M' George Innes Presbyter in Aberdeen was consecrated Bishop of Brechen at Alloa, by Bp Falconar Primus, Bp Rose & Bp Petrie.

1782. Sept. 25. M' John Skinner Presbyter in Aberdeen, was consecrated Bishop Co-adjutor, at Luthermuir in the Diocese of Brechen, by Bp Kilgour Primus, Bp Rose, & Bp Petrie.

That this is a just List of the Consecrations of the Bishops in Scotland since the Year One Thousand six hundred & eighty-eight, so far as the order of Consecration is concerned, is attested by

ARTHUR PETRIE,
Clerk to the Synod of Bishops.[1]

[1] And then Bishop of Ross and Caithness.

1784. *Nov.* 14. *Dr. Samuel Seabury, Presbyter, from the State of Connecticut, in America, was consecrated Bishop, at Aberdeen, by Bishop Kilgour, Primus, Bishop Petrie and Bishop Skinner. The deed of consecration is as follows:*

IN DEI NOMINE. Amen.

Omnibus ubique Catholicis per Presentes pateat,
NOS, Robertum Kilgour, miseratione divina, Episcopum Aberdonien — Arthurum Petrie, Episcopum Rossen et Moravien — et Joannem Skinner, Episcopum Coadjutorem; Mysteria Sacra Domini nostri Jesu Christi in Oratorio supradicti Joannis Skinner apud Aberdoniam celebrantes, Divini Numinis Præsidio fretos (presentibus tam e Clero quam e Populo testibus idoneis) Samuelem Seabury, Doctorem Divinitatis, sacro Presbyteratus ordine jam decoratum ac nobis præ Vitæ integritate, Morum probitate et Orthodoxia, commendatum, et ad docendum et regendum aptum et idonium, ad sacrum et sublimem Episcopatus Ordinem promovisse, et rite ac canonice, secundum Morem et Ritus Ecclesiæ Scoticanæ, consecrasse, Die Novembris decimo quarto, Anno Æræ Christianæ Millesimo Septingentisimo Octagesimo Quarto.——

> In cujus Rei Testimonium, Instrumento huic (chirographis nostris prius munito) Sigilla nostra apponi mandavimus.

ROBERTUS KILGOUR, Episcopus, et Primus. (L. S.)
ARTHURUS PETRIE, Episcopus. (L. S.)
JOANNES SKINNER, Episcopus. (L. S.)

www.ingramcontent.com/pod-product-compliance
Lightning Source LLC
Chambersburg PA
CBHW020156170426
43199CB00010B/1070